REVISIONIST MARXISM:
THE OPPOSITION WITHIN

Ralph M. Faris

Philosophical Currents

Vol. 7

David H. DeGrood

Editor

Edward D'Angelo
Marvin Farber
Mitchell Franklin
Stuart L. Hackel
Donald C. Hodges

James Lawler
Benjamin B. Page
Dale Riepe
Shingo Shibata
William G. Stratton

Associates

The important views expressed by our writers are represented without necessarily implying concurrence of either editors or publisher.

B. R. GRÜNER B. V. Amsterdam-1974

Revisionist Marxism:
The Opposition within

by

Ralph M. Faris

B. R. GRÜNER B.V. Amsterdam 1974

Library of Congress Catalog
Card Number 73-78902

ISBN 90 6032 017 4

© 1974 by B.R. Grüner B.V. Amsterdam, Netherlands

TABLE OF CONTENTS

Chapter I

THE RESURGENCE OF REVISIONISM

(a) *The New Critical Theory*

The "undogmatic ones" have closed ranks in order to "save socialism". The "progressive communists" sound the charge and the bourgeois papers, to whom communist authors – at least "orthodox ones" – stand reservedly in opposition, show their colors for the pugnacious warriors. And then they inveigh against the "true" Marxists who really are still Marxists, but it is just that they permit no yoke to be attached – which bourgeois journalist cannot sympathize with them on that?

"Dogmatism, doctrinairism", "ossification of the party – the inevitable retribution that follows the violent strait-lacing of thought", – so quoted Lenin about his contemporary "anti-dogmatic ones" – "these are the enemies against which the kindly champions of 'freedom of criticism' are allying their forces". And he continues, "We are very glad that this question has been brought up and we would propose only to add to it another question: 'Who are to be the judges?'"[1]

The "anti-dogmatic ones" against whom Lenin (quoted by Roland Lang above) debates, and who are the subject of this book, are making their presence known today in an apparent proliferation of anti-Soviet, anti-Marxist, anti-"Stalinist", anti-proletarian writings and publications. In their writings, etc., they argue, appeal, and exhort, as if *they* were, in fact, the judges. For the international socialist movement, this has resulted in severe and constant criticism of the Communist parties in all socialist countries, as well as in persistent barrages of anti-Soviet sentiment. Soviet Marxism-Leninism, notwithstanding all its transformations and modifications, is being subjected to deeply penetrating questions of purpose and content. Such notables as Henri Lefebvre, Roger Garaudy, Leszek Kolakowski, Ota Šik, Ernst Fischer, Franz Marek, Karel Kosík, Gajo Petrović, Svetozar Stojanović, Robert Havamann, Milovan Djilas, Ivan Svitak, Herbert Marcuse, and others, have been rebuked and labeled "revisionists" by the Communist Parties of the Soviet Union and other East European, socialist countries. In addition, because of the theoretical and ideological vacuum of bourgeois society, there is a tendency for the thoughts of these writers to become the *semi-official stance* in the West. These intellectuals also tend to become isolated from

---

1. Roland Lang, "How Original Are the 'Undogmatic Marxists'?," *Marxistische Blätter*, (January/February, 1971), p. 80.

workers' movements and to develop their thought exclusively for other intellectuals – much the same as do modern theorists of Western bourgeois social sciences.

But how did these scholars, intellectuals, scientists, and philosophers come to be considered as "revisionists"? Are they simply the rejuvenators of the original revisionist thinkers such as Eduard Bernstein[2] and Karl Kautsky,[3] or rather, do they reflect an increasing dissatisfaction of people living under socialist governments? Does it represent, as well, part of the *immanent dialectic* of Marxist theory in relationship to the *rapid development* of socialist society? Can one not expect much more dissent and criticism as the international communist movement commits itself, both internally and externally (within parties or between parties), to various positions in regard to the various contingencies of upcoming world-historical events? Upon what major theoretical and practical categories do they distinguish themselves, e.g., from the "official" interpretation of Marxism? What are their prospects for "success", given the status of intellectuals and the background of the leaders in these countries, in terms of a growing opposition in Eastern Europe? What implications, if any, can be found in the views of such opposing voices for social theory and praxis?

In attempting to provide explanations for the above pockets of dissent within the Marxist intellectual community, I shall be concerned with the characteristics of the status of intellectuals, the historical dimensions of this specific intellectual role vis-à-vis that of their American counterparts, and the impact of their incessant and vociferous critiques. The subject of this book is of vital concern to both Marxist and non-Marxist alike for the following reasons:

(1) Eastern Europe has, historically, represented fertile ground for the development of both socio-political theories and real social movements which have actually altered the social and political structures of many countries. One might remember that Europe, especially Eastern Europe, has been the battleground for two major world wars in this century alone, and therefore can be expected to be a hotbed of political and social activity. Thus, the rich historical heritage and obvious political potential of the ideas emanating from this section of the world must be considered in any evaluation or investigation of possible future developments both in Europe and across the globe.[4]

(2) Politically, the areas from which the most vicious as well as constructive criticisms can be heard are defined as emerging socialist countries. If

2. For a presentation of Bernstein's development, see Christian Gneuss, "The Precursor: Edward Bernstein", in Leopold Labedz, ed., *Revisionism* (New York: Praeger, 1962).
3. For the classic refutation of Kautsky, see V. I. Lenin, *The Proletarian Revolution and the Renegade Kautsky* (New York: International).
4. Cf. Scott Nearing, *The Making of a Radical* (New York: Harper and Row, 1972), p. 239.

then the operation of these socialist states can be considered as experimental and instructive, the observations and comments by their members, indeed, even the most tendentious and disruptive, may provide analysts and revolutionaries with some significant indications as to the status of those experiments. In the mind of Scott Nearing, the socialist countries of Eastern Europe represent a unique historical trend. He writes:

> American socialists, like their European comrades, assumed that as capitalism matured and declined it would be replaced by a socialist pattern of society. Europe was therefore the grandstand seat for anyone concerned with this revolutionary aspect of social development. Europe was not only the homeland of capitalism, it was likewise the birthplace of the modern labor movement, the modern cooperative movement and the present-day socialist-communist political movements. The real attraction therefore, for an American socialist in Europe, was not the deathbed scene of expiring monopoly capitalism but the emergence on the European stage of the infant socialist republics.
> . . .Europe was therefore a vast sociological laboratory in which several hundred million people were carrying on social experiments that were bound to have a profound influence on the future of Europeans and a lesser but consequent influence on the future of the whole human race.[5]

It should be noted, then, before we examine the "new critical theories" of the revisionists, that by almost every indication used to measure the success of new systems of government, GNP, standard of living, industrial output, infant mortality rates, public education facilities, medical care, etc., the Eastern European countries have made tremendous progress.[6]

(b) *The First Case against Revisionism: The G.D.R.*

Since one of the major points of my refutation of much of what has become known as revisionist writing and obscurantism rests squarely upon the phenomenal advances made in the very socialist countries so unjustifiably criticized and abused, for the most part by the "new Marxists", it would not be nappropriate to cite some of the major indicators mentioned above. Thus,

5. *Ibid.*, p. 239.
6. For some of the criteria used to assess the quality of life in any society, see the chapter entitled, "The Quality of Monopoly Capitalist Society", in Paul A. Baran and Paul M. Sweezy's *Monopoly Capital* (New York: Monthly Review, 1967), pp. 281–335. [Sweezy, it can be pointed out, has more and more tended towards the Chinese side of the Russo-Chinese split, as he has recently spoken of "social-imperialism" in connection with the U.S.S.R.'s policies (*Monthly Review*, vol. 23, # 10, p.7f).] Also, see *Monthly Review* (vol. 24, # 5, p. 10) for a discussion of valid indicators for measuring real development within countries. In addition, for the actual statistics concerning the development of the East European states, see the *United Nations Demographic Yearbook* (1948–1972) and *The Statistical Yearbook of the United Nations*, (1948–1972). And John Dornberg's *The Other Germany* offers resounding proof of the success steadily accruing to such socialist countries. Finally, for the latest study of the G.D.R. and its attempts to erase the mark of racism from its land, see Claude M. Lightfoot's *Racism and Human Survival*.

in terms of the quality of life considerations, so often lamented by the revisionists, we find, by checking the actual figures for infant mortality rates of both the United States and the G.D.R., the following:

	1953	1962	1963	1964	1965	1966	1967	1968
G.D.R.	53.5	31.6	31.4	28.8	24.8	22.8	21.4	20.4
U.S.	27.8	25.3	25.2	24.8	24.7	23.7	22.4	21.7
F.D.R.	46.4	29.2	26.9	25.2	23.8	23.5	22.8	22.8

Sources: United Nations Statistical Yearbook, 1969, United Nations Statistical Office, New York, 1969.

In the space of only fifteen years, the G.D.R. has not only reduced its infant mortality rate from 53.5 per 1000 live births as compared with the United States' 27.8 figure, to 20.4 per 1000 live births as compared to the United States' 21.7 figure, but has surpassed the most powerful imperialist nation in the world as well.

Taking another significant consideration of progress we discover these revealing medical care statistics:

Item	U.S.	U.S.S.R.	G.D.R.
Hospitals	7,172	26,428	679
Beds	1,671,125	2,397,900	198,513
Population per bed	120	100	80
Physicians	305,453	550,389	24,620
Population per physician	650	430	650

Sources: United Nations Statistical Yearbook, 1969, United Nations Statistical Office, New York, 1969.

As the chart illustrates, both the U.S.S.R. and the G.D.R. possess decisive advantages in important categories of health care.

In his comprehensive and well documented study of the G.D.R. in 1968, John Dornberg cites many figures pointing to the continuing, progressive character of East Germany's economic programs. Without reservations he writes:

And where is East Germany today?
It has the highest standard of living in the Communist world, and is the world's eighth largest industrial power. Its gross national product and industrial productivity are growing faster than Russia's, West Germany's, Britain's, France's and Italy's. It ranks among the world's top ten producers of electric power, artificial gas, chemical fibres and fertilizers, synthetic rubber, railway rolling stock,

merchant ships, radio and TV receivers, household appliances, industrial machinery, machine tools, and optical and precision instruments.

Despite the initial disadvantages with which it started, the G.D.R. has built nine new major power plants, one of them the largest in Europe; fifteen iron and steel mills; eight chemical and twelve machine tool factories; four shipyards; seven new electro-technical and optical plants; six cement works and eight basic complexes for raw materials conversion including the world's only lignite coking combine.

Since the end of 1960 East Germany's national income has increased by 26 percent at an average annual rate of 3.7 percent. The gross national product has increased by almost 46 percent, the industrial productivity by nearly 45 percent.[7]

Dornberg is not finished examining the ascent of the East German social system as he continues to contrast the F.R.G. with the G.D.R. – this time in terms of educational institutions:

Both Germanys entered the postwar period with the same system of education. West Germany's remained essentially unchanged. What transpired in the G.D.R. however is nothing less than a pedagogic explosion....

Whereas only 30 percent of West German youths receive ten or more years of schooling, in the G.D.R. this group represents more than 70 percent. Only 4.3 percent of West German youths go on to college. In the G.D.R. it is already 15 percent and Ulbricht has promised that it will be 25 percent by 1970. The number of East German universities and colleges has increased from six, at the end of the war, to forty-four in 1967 with another thousand specialized institutes, including 212 technical schools of higher learning. The total number of university and college students in East Germany in 1967 was 110,000 plus 129,000 in technical schools compared to a total of 288,000 in West Germany whose population is 3.5 times larger.[8]

Finally, lest one might conclude that all of the above progress has been achieved at the expense of a healthy diet, Dornberg writes:

East Germany's per acreage grain yield now matches West Germany's, the root crop gap is being closed. Though the GDR's human population is less than one-third that of West Germany's, its livestock population is almost half as large. Meat production is now high enough to provide each East German with 128 pounds per year – just five pounds less than the per capita West German consumption. Though butter remains rationed in East Germany, the actual annual per capita consumption in the GDR – 27.5 pounds is higher than West Germany's – 18.7 pounds... for the first time in 1966 the East German milk yield surpassed 3000 kilograms (6600 pounds) per cow.[9]

7. John Dornberg, *The Other Germany* (New York: Doubleday, 1968), pp. 135–136.
8. *Ibid.*, p. 309.
9. *Ibid.*, pp. 192–193.

All of this has not been accomplished by ignoring or de-emphasizing other aspects of East German life. The G.D.R.'s intentions are to provide for an environment which will allow the individual maximum opportunity to develop both his physical and mental faculties in cooperative association with the members of his society. In terms of those mental or creative aspirations, the G.D.R. has truly dedicated itself to the realization of the socialist personality. Perhaps Bernt von Kugelgen, editor-in-chief of *Sonntag*, a G.D.R. cultural periodical, provides us with a clearer picture of just what that personality would be engaged in in the G.D.R.. He writes:

> There is hardly a work team in our industry that has not joined the "work, learn and live in a socialist way" movement. More than 75 percent of these teams have arranged special cultural and educational plans for themselves in which the workers pose firm and obligatory goals for further vocational and social science qualifications. This includes going to theaters, concerts and museums, and fostering the partnership relations with artists. The teams, as bodies commissioning literary or musical works, cooperate with confidence and in a comradely way with writers and composers, discuss with them, bring them closer to their world and also learn from them. Let me quote you a few figures. There are 30,704 artistic working groups in the G.D.R. with 558,828 members, including: 4,143 amateur orchestras with 66,939 musicians; 6,496 choirs with 294,402 singers; 1,147 amateur theaters with 15,274 performers; 1,888 circles for pictorial art with 27,589 participants.[10]

Wilfried Nonnewitz, adding another dimension to the model of socialist man pursued by the G.D.R., discusses the theater there and its impact:

> During the past year the approximately 100 G.D.R. theaters counted roughly 12.2 million spectators. This means that the number of spectators increased by half a million since 1966. The present trend as well is one of growth. Before 1966 there had been a reduction in the number of spectators.
> Spectator interest is aroused mostly by contemporary plays and by classical humanist drama. A total of 3.8 million spectators attended such performances in 1970.[11]

In dealing with the question of racism and the way in which the G.D.R. as well as other socialist countries are determined to eradicate it, Claude M. Lightfoot's *Racism and Human Survival* compares the educational materials (textbooks, teachers, etc.), among other indicators, of the G.D.R. with those of the F.R.G. and the United States. His examples prove quite easily the assertion that only in capitalist societies is racism encouraged by the bourgeoisie in their efforts to maintain their power and profit. Nothing could

10. Bernt Von Kugelgen, "Culture and Humanism, GDR", *New World Review*, vol. 40, #3, Summer, 1972, pp. 47–48.
11. Wilfried Nonnewitz, "GDR Theater and Its Public", *New World Review*, vol. 40, #3, Summer, 1972, pp. 48–49.

illustrate this more perfectly than comparing the actual textbooks used in grade schools in both capitalist and socialist countries.[12]

My reasoning in presenting the preceding tables, statistics and descriptions of the G.D.R., as well as of the U.S.S.R., revolves around the slick, aberrant, and quite often highly abstract intellectual theories and perspectives employed by the "new revisionists" to discredit the monumental advances achieved by the socialist states espousing the basic principles of Marxism-Leninism. It is my hope that the foregoing *facts* will, in some major way, convince the reader of the factual bankruptcy of the modern revisionists' critiques of their respective countries. The revisionists incessantly babble about the lack of any serious progress in these Eastern European countries, as well as in the U.S.S.R. Even if one finds such a critique false, this is not to deny, of course, any *serious* problems or shortcomings associated with building socialism in the Eastern European states during the last 25 years.

Finally, it should be noted that the above quality of life considerations (health care, mortality rates, industrial production, educational standards, etc.) are considered important not only by socialist countries but by all members of the United Nations; the U.N. publishes yearly, quarterly, and monthly, a host of statistics using the very same categories mentioned above. A man must have food, shelter, medical care and work *before* he can move on to more complex theoretical or practical problems. Therefore, these quality of life considerations are significant instruments to be used in measuring the advances made by any country.

(c) *The Intensification of Revisionism in an Age of Acute Crisis*

There is a comparatively unified platform on which the critiques and theories of modern revisionists rest. The *leading role* of the communist party both in Eastern Europe and in the U.S.S.R. is so defined and historically established that there is little doubt today who the revisionists are. The central core of revisionist thinking, although subtle and obscurantist in form, can be distinguished from objectively established Marxism-Leninism.

Thus, there appear to be two major tenets around which these dissenters are able to gather: First, that Leninism is *not* the further development of Marxism, but a specifically *Russian phenomenon*, and thus there is a need to "return" to the genuine Marx; second, that socialism in the Soviet Union and other socialist states is at variance with Marx's theory, representing a bureaucratic-étatist distortion of socialism, and thus revolutionaries must devise a new "model", combining socialism with democracy and freedom.[13] The revisionists advance arguments which insist that the transference of old

12. Claude M. Lightfoot, *Racism and Human Survival* (New York: International, 1972), pp. 137–157.
13. Cf. Alfred Kosing, "Modern Revisionism: Philosophical and Socio-Political Functions", *World Marxist Review* (March, 1971), pp. 115–117.

concepts to *completely new situations* creates distrust and division within the ranks of the workers' movements in socialist countries, and that the diversity of tradition, of economic and political development, and the different stages in the development of socialist parties and societies indicate the need to utilize a *variety* of methods in dealing with the contemporary problems and struggles confronting modern socialist states. This need for diversity takes the form of conflicting views and assessments on a number of persistent and highly troublesome propositions, *alienation* being one of those most often mentioned.

However, in order to clarify the rather unique but obfuscating historical role of the "new Marxist" revisionist thinker and critic, it should be noted that the theoretical and empirical content, as well as the ideological sources, of the objections and criticisms of the "opposition within" differ substantially from the old revisionism of Bernstein, *et al*. While Bernsteinian revisionism openly proclaimed its departure from the historical and economic laws established by Marx and rejected the dialectics of the class struggle, one newer revisionist stream emphasizes returning to the *young* Marx as necessary for salvaging what remains of a "deteriorating and stagnating revolution". In abandoning, for the most part, the present status of the dictatorship of the proletariat, these self-styled "rescuers" of Marxist thought resort to an idealistic emphasis on the inner man (e.g. Marcuse). This belief has been translated into an ever-increasing hostility to Marxist-Leninist philosophy.

Another type of revisionism, the Yugoslav variety, places its emphasis on decentralization and quasi-syndicalist schemes, mainly in opposition to its so-called "Stalinist" neighbors, large and small. Thus, the League of Yugoslav Communists enunciate their differences:

> The first is the phenomenon of bureaucracy and statism. Closely related to this phenomenon is the tendency towards ideological monopoly, as well as the attempt to transform Marxist thought – which can retain its vitality and revolutionary character only by being continually developed on the basis of practice and experience – into a static collection of rigid dogmas and abstract truths, adjusted to meet certain temporary needs. Therein lies the source of contemporary dogmatism and the attempts to carry out specific statist-pragmatic revisions of the determined scientific postulates of Marxism-Leninism.[14]

With respect to the role of the proletariat, both historically and politically, the League has this to say:

> What is most important in all this is the fact that the working class cannot become master of its own fate, and consequently the main driving force of social

14. "Yugoslav Ideological Innovations", Excerpts from the Programme of the League of Yugoslav Communists (Belgrade, 1958), in *Communist Political Systems*, ed. Alvin Z. Rubinstein (Prentice-Hall, 1966), p. 96.

progress, unless it secures direct control over management of production and distribution. In this function, no *regime* of state control over the private owner, no state machinery or state manager, can be substituted for the working class.[15]

Bernstein's revisionism, in contrast, had attacked revolutionary action and critical dialectics, and supported parliamentary reform; the dialectical materialist philosophy was passed over, in a reformist and reactionary way, for a Neo-Kantian theory of knowledge and ethics. In this way, the basic tenets of Marxism revolving around the class struggle were discarded for a purely "ethical" ideal.

Given the contemporary problems of today's socialist states in Eastern Europe, it is not surprising that the "new Marxists" have sought *alternative* philosophical and epistemological bases and concepts. These theoretical foundations and roots, Kosing states, are used in an attempt to establish

an interpretive generalization of man's historical activity and... have been influenced to a greater or lesser degree by Marxism. This applies to the socio-critical theory of the 'Frankfurt school' (T. Adorno, M. Horkheimer, J. Habermas), the related views of Marcuse, the philosophical anthropology of Fromm, ...the existentialism of Jean-Paul Sartre, the 'philosophy of hope' of E. Bloch...[16]

On the basis of their abstract humanistic philosophy of man, centered around man's alienation from his social structure, such writers maintain that alienation is a universal phenomenon, and that, until all of the secrets of knowledge and human activity are uncovered, it will remain an anthropological category (i.e. the nature of alienation is rooted in man, not his social structure), vanishing perhaps sometime in the distant future.[17] Their conclusion that man is as alienated and deformed under socialism as in capitalism is reached indirectly through their evaluation of the trends towards increasing "bureaucratization" and centralization (both of which are prime sources, according to the "new Marxists", of alienation) within *both* kinds of society.

Moreover, because of the "false hopes" produced by socialist revolutions and the resulting social schisms in socialist societies, they feel that alienation is still pronounced and oppressive therein. Professor Mihailo Marković of the Philosophy Department of the University of Belgrade expresses his dissatisfaction over the post-revolutionary situation of formerly revolutionary movements when he writes:

Another surprising and indeed alarming 20th century experience is an obvious deterioration of motives and a sharp moral decay within the leadership of many victorious revolutionary movements. For most ordinary participants of those

15. *Ibid.*, p. 99.
16. Kosing, *op. cit.*, p. 119.
17. Cf. *ibid.*, p. 117.

15

movements the phenomenon was so astounding that they never grasped what happened. By now the sociological dimensions of this process is clear: it is the transformation of the revolutionary avant-garde into a privileged elite, and it takes place whenever the society as a whole is not sufficiently developed and integrated.[18]

It is upon such an interpretation of man and alienation today that many of the "opposition within" construct their theoretical framework. Such East European philosophers agitate amidst the most liberal of socialist environments yet, positing an ideal man and an ideal socialism, counterposing it to the socialism of the Soviet Union, the G.D.R., and other Eastern European countries.

Whether it is intentional or not, the "new revisionists", defenders of the "true" Marx, may, in some cases, be preparing the ground for anti-socialist and counter-revolutionary forces by acting as an ideological and philosophical *vehicle* of counter-revolution. Subjectively, on the other hand, these dissenters are in a theoretical and empirical quandary. They can embrace neither the philosophical and political foundations, and contradictions, of the Western world of capitalism (at least not *officially*) nor the "dogmatic" (by their standards) ideology and political control of the Marxist-Leninist "bureaucrat".

Although the principle of Communist Party unity, so essential to the progress of socialism, is still very much the official policy, the role of the "new revisionists" in criticizing and undercutting official government policies poses various difficulties for their respective parties. Historically and politically, to be sure, there are also striking similarities between the Western intellectuals' political opposition and that of the "new Marxists".

Thus, before examining the ideological arguments and theories of the "new wave of revisionists", it will be fruitful to explore the possibilities, in terms of roles, for intellectuals, social scientists, artists, etc., in the particular social orders in which they live. One of my intentions in this study is to demonstrate the intense sense of alienation and frustration experienced by the "new critical thinkers" within their own social structure, and to link these feelings with their faulty conceptions of their roles as intellectuals, etc., in it.

18. Mihailo Marković, "Human Nature and Social Development", in *Contemporary East European Philosophy*, ed. Edward D'Angelo, *et al.* (Spartacus Books, 1970), I, p. 32.

Chapter II

THE NATURE AND ROLES OF INTELLECTUALS

(a) *Bourgeois versus Socialist Conceptions*

Thus, the supreme function of bourgeois philosophy is to obscure the miseries of contemporary reality: the spiritual destitution of vast numbers of men, the fundamental dichotomy in their consciousness, and the increasingly intolerable disparity between what they could achieve and what little they have actually accomplished. This philosophy conceals the true nature of bourgeois rule. ...It is a weapon in the struggle against the anger and the spirit of revolt now manifesting themselves. It serves to divert the exploited from the contemplation of their own degradation and debasement – an activity that might prove dangerous to the exploiters. Its mission is to gain universal acceptance for the established order by making it palatable, by confering upon it a certain nobility, and by furnishing rationalizations for its every aspect. It mystifies the victims of the bourgeois regime, all those who might some day rise up against it. It leads them into culs-de-sac where their rebellious instincts will be extinguished. It is the faithful servant of that social class which is the cause of all the degradation in the world today, the very class to which the philosophers themselves belong. In a word, the purpose of this philosophy is to explain, to fortify, and to propagate the half-truths manufactured by the bourgeoisie and so useful in consolidating its power.[1]

In thus defining the distorted, historically constant role of bourgeois intellectuals, Nizan, above, has established, albeit negatively, the revolutionary or historically necessary function of intellectuals, or simply, that which a philosopher *ought* not to be. In this powerful exposé of the history of philosophy and the roles of its agents, we discover Nizan's compelling and forceful theme: that philosophers, intellectuals, etc., have either directly or indirectly, consciously or unconsciously, defended or supported the ruling class in its domination over the proletariat, that these academic whores have consistently championed the interests of the established order over the rights of man. And like the prostitute who knows that there is something immoral if not illegal about her profession, these men of letters conceal their real intentions. Nizan spots their covertness:

But only bourgeois have a real need for subtlety in their classifications and palpable profundity in their intellectual exercises, because they alone have some-

1. Paul Nizan, *The Watchdogs: Philosophers and the Established Order* (New York: Monthly Review, 1971), pp. 91–92.

thing to hide – and vulgarity is a much less effective mask than subtlety and nuance. The profundity of the philosophy can be judged by the shape and thickness of the cloud.[2]

After attempting, therefore, to bring Nizan's book up-to-date with respect to the most current bourgeois nonsense and rationalizations used to defend the capitalist order, I hope to demonstrate some of the more obvious links between revisionist critics and intellectuals and bourgeois philosophers, etc., the former sometimes being more of a threat to socialist societies than the latter.

Unable or unwilling, then, to confront the social conflict inherent in their societies, bourgeois scholars and social scientists find themselves in both a philosophical and sociological predicament. But before we examine the difficulties they encounter in establishing their role, let us first attempt to discover, in a general way, the roots of their dilemma in the superstructure of capitalist societies.

Although there is among Western theorists considerable controversy over the subject-matter to be investigated and the methods of investigating, there is *relative* consensus as to the role and disposition of an intellectual. To Christopher Lasch the intellectual is

> ...a person for whom thinking fulfills at once the function of work and play;
> ...a person whose relationship to society is defined, both in his eyes and in the eyes of the society, principally by his presumed capacity to comment upon it with greater detachment than those more directly caught up in the practical business of production and power. Because his vocation is to be a critic of society, in the most general sense, and because the value of his criticism is presumed to rest on a measure of detachment from the current scene, the intellectual's relation to the rest of society is never entirely comfortable....[3]

Edward Shils also has a comment on the "alienative" status of intellectuals.

> In all societies, even those in which the intellectuals are notable for their conservatism, the diverse paths of creativity, as well as an inevitable tendency towards negativism, impel a partial rejection of the prevailing system of cultural values. The very process of elaboration and development involves a measure of rejection.[4]

And finally, from the grand obcurantist himself, Talcott Parsons, we receive the following cryptic message:

> In this setting I should like to speak of the intellectual as a person who, though as a member of a society in the nature of the case he performs a complex of social

2. *Ibid.*, p. 40.
3. Christopher Lasch, *The New Radicalism in America* (New York: Knopf, 1966), p. ix.
4. Edward Shils, "The Intellectuals and the Powers", *On Intellectuals*, ed. Philip Rieff (New York: Doubleday, 1969), p. 30.

roles, is in his principal role-capacity expected – an expectation normally shared by himself – to put cultural considerations above social in defining the commitments by virtue of which his primary role and positions are significant as contributions to valued outcomes of his action.[5]

Indeed, whether the intellectual is a philosopher, an artist, a scientist, a writer, etc., in the view of the Western "functionalist" theorists (T. Parsons, Shils, Merton), his relationship to the "masses" must be either superior or uneasy or both – I translate this to mean antagonistic or apologetic, much the same as Nizan, mentioned earlier, viewed bourgeois philosophers. Actually then, there are two aspects to their viewpoints on intellectuals. They must, by virtue of their constant analysis, from their lofty positions at the right hand of the ruling classes, of the social, economic and political institutions of their societies, be deeply and objectively opposed to the societal value-system and structural arrangements, but powerless to change or alter them, or, by virtue of their more "professional" approach (and "objective", "scientific", "value-free" method), be neutral to the power bases of society, thereby insuring the "autonomy" of the intellectual. Historically, it appears as if the latter was a reaction to, or product of, the former. The perils of public rejection and anger, however, do not seem to have precipitated the American or Western intellectual's flight to *value-free* territory as much as the ruling élite's disapproval and threatened withdrawal of security in the form of tenure, research grants, and prestigeful government positions. As Gouldner, in reference to one field within the social sciences in America, explains:

> The value-free image of social science is not consciously held for expedience's sake; it is not contrived deliberately as a hedge against public displeasure. It could not function as a face-saving device if it were. What seems more likely is that it entails something in the nature of a tacit bargain: in return for a measure of autonomy and social support, many social scientists have surrendered their critical impulses. This was not usually a callous "sell-out" but a slow process of mutual accommodation; both parties suddenly found themselves betrothed without out a formal ceremony.[6]

In his latest book, depicting the bankrupt state of American sociology, Gouldner underscores this theme again in the spirit of Nizan:

> In one part, then, the dominant expressions of the academic social sciences embody an accommodation to the alienation of men in contemporary society, rather than a determined effort to transcend it. The core concepts of society and culture, as held by the social sciences, entail the view that their autonomy and

---

5. Talcott Parsons, "The Intellectual", *On Intellectuals*, p. 4.
6. Alvin Gouldner, "Anti-Minotaur: The Myth of a Value-Free Sociology", *The New Sociology*, ed. Irving Louis Horowitz (New York: Oxford University Press, 1964), p. 207.

uncontrollability are a normal and natural condition, rather than intrinsically a kind of pathology. It is this assumption that is at the heart of the *repressive* component of sociology.[7]

Thus in either case, the intellectual basically is alienated from the masses, from the working population – the very groups he desperately needs in order to maintain an accurate perspective and appraisal of his social order; in addition, it is postulated by these same theorists that there is no longer a *need* for the social scientists to take a side, or to position themselves opposite anyone in the social structure, as, we are told, new levels of progress and harmony have been achieved. Many intellectuals moved into this unapplied quagmire after accepting the tacit agreement relating to their cooperation with the ruling élites – this process has often been referred to as the cooption thesis. Thus, true to form, S. M. Lipset, prominent rationalizer for the status quo, comments upon the new "harmony":

> This change in Western political life reflects the fact that the fundamental problems of the industrial revolution have been solved.... This very triumph of the democratic social revolution in the West ends domestic politics for those intellectuals who must have ideologies or utopias to motivate them to political action.[8]

Clearly this position either ignores or glosses over the major contradictions of capitalist societies, and confirms what Nizan offers in the opening quote of this chapter. There are, of course, those who have rejected the means and goals of capitalist society and ideology; nonetheless, they resist or resent any alignment with working people, political movements or causes, and are in a priggish, curse-on-both-your-houses frame of mind, content to spin off their theories or "facts", research designs or theses, as if there really were some convergence of ideologies. What social theorists must struggle against is the continual attempt by other analysts and ideologists, such as Shils, Parsons, Lipset, etc., to maintain that the various alternative stances of intellectuals are either universal or inevitable. Here the potent rebuttal of Georg Lukács, to be mentioned later, will suffice. Lukács talks about the naïve or dishonest explanations offered by theorists such as the ones mentioned above; he uses as his example the historian, Arnold Toynbee:

> Or take Toynbee, for example. His book is the greatest success in the philosophy of history since Spengler. He investigates the growth and decline of all known cultures and comes to the conclusion that neither the control of natural forces, nor the control of social conditions is capable of influencing this process; he also attempts to prove that all efforts to influence the course of development through

7. Alvin Gouldner, *The Coming Crisis of Western Sociology* (New York: Basic Books, 1970), p. 53.
8. Seymour Martin Lipset, *The Political Man* (New York: Anchor, 1963). Cited by Gil Green, *The New Radicalism* (New York: International, 1971), p. 29.

the use of force (i.e., all revolutions) are a priori condemned to failure. Twenty-one cultures have already perished. One solitary culture, the West European, has continually grown up to now because, at its inception, Jesus discovered this new, non-violent path of renewal. And today? Toynbee summarizes his first six volumes to the effect that God – whose nature is just as constant as man's – will not deny us a new deliverance if only we ask for it with sufficient humility.

It seems to me that the most fanatic exponent of atomic war in the U.S.A. could desire nothing better than for the progressive intellectuals to do nothing more than pray for such a favor, while he himself can organize the atomic war undisturbed.[9] [Or napalm the Vietnamese, etc., with harmony.]

In socialist countries the development and activities of the social sciences are considered as consistent with the goals of the members of the society. There is no artificially created, nor historically contrived, hostility between scholars and society as there is in countries like the United States. Writes A. I. Paskov, a corresponding member of the U.S.S.R's Academy of Sciences:

In the Soviet Union there are two classes: the workers and the collective farm peasantry. Intellectual workers, the Soviet intelligentsia, form a special social group; they are recruited from the people themselves, they serve the people and work together *with* them [my italics]. The relations between the workers and the collective-farm peasantry, as well as between these two classes and the Soviet intelligentsia, are those of friendly co-operation and mutual help between people free from exploitation.[10]

Paskov then explains the role of the social sciences in the U.S.S.R. as being "indissolubly connected with the whole of the social, economic and political structure of Soviet society".[11] This last statement, however, does not seem to contradict one aspect of the relationship of bourgeois intellectual to their social order, namely one of direct or indirect justification of the status quo, of the existing socio-politico-economic relationships in capitalist societies. Even so, it is becoming increasingly more difficult, both analytically and objectively, for the American intellectual establishment, in the wake of events such as Vietnam, the Pentagon Papers, etc., to dream up credible systems of belief to match popular discontent. Noting the qualitatively different functions of the social sciences under capitalism and socialism, Paskov accounts, too, for any similarities:

The development of the social sciences is [a] strictly logical process. The social sciences are one of the forms of social consciousness, of the ideology of society,

9. Georg Lukács, "On the Responsibility of the Intellectuals", *Telos*, vol. 2, No. 1, Spring, 1969, pp. 126–127.
10. A. I. Paskov, "Observations Concerning the Social Sciences in the U.S.S.R.", *Social Sciences in the U.S.S.R.*, International Social Science Council (New York: Basic Books, 1965), p. 2.
11. *Ibid.*, p. 2.

parallel with the natural sciences and other forms of social consciousness such as art, religion, etc. According to Marxist methodology, the social sciences deal with the superstructure of society, together with other forms of ideology and with the political institutions of a country. The superstructure of society, including also the social sciences, is in the final analysis determined, regarding its ideological content and forms, by the basis of society – its economic structure. . . .
Class ideologists, preoccupied with preserving antiquated and obsolete forms of social life, employ conservative and reactionary ideas and doctrines in their struggle with the progressive social forces, whereas the ideologists of the progressive classes, concerned with eliminating old systems and establishing new ones, employ advanced and progressive ideas and theories.
The close connection between the social sciences and the economy, the class struggle and the political system, imparts a class character to these sciences.
It follows that in a bourgeois society, divided into antagonistic classes, there is a very large variety of social science theories, serving the different economic, political and ideological interests of those classes.[12]

The eminent Marxist scholar, J. D. Bernal, perhaps specifies with distinct clarity the profound, humanistic tasks to which intellectuals, scientists, etc., dedicate their efforts in socialist countries as compared with the desperate and clandestine activities of the Western world's intellectual parasites, when he comments:

. . . That science [in socialist societies] is given the task of helping to . . . [satisfy] ascertainable human needs for shelter, for means of production and transport; and secondly, that science is ceasing to be something separated from the rest of social activities and the preserve of an intellectual élite, and is becoming part of the everyday life and work of the great majority of the population.
This is very different from the position under capitalism. Under capitalism science is limited in academic circles to diluted and unco-ordinated contributions to the understanding of nature. In practice it is applied when it is profitable to do so or where it can produce lethal weapons. There is a violent refusal to treat science as a whole and to relate its various parts in any comprehensive plan of human betterment. Such a plan would in effect be completely nonsensical in a capitalist country, because it would be absurd to even think of planning science, when production itself remains subject to the whims of private property and monopoly which restricts it except for military ends. But in a socialist state this restriction is removed and science falls naturally into its place as the normal means of improving productivity in a continuous and progressive way.[13]

Given all of this contrast in the basic directions of the social sciences or sciences in general, one can begin to understand that the rationale for the function and role of Western theorists is colored by their class connections and political leanings, which is to say that, considering the exploitive relation-

12. *Ibid.*, pp. 1–2.
13. J. D. Bernal, *Marx and Science* (New York: International, 1952), pp. 42–43.

22

ships between capitalists and the clearer-thinking working classes, the actions and activities of the former being justified and defended by Western theorists, it is not beyond instant comprehension to discover the discomfort experienced by the intellectual when dealing with working class populations; nor is it difficult to understand his subsequent resort to concepts explaining the "neutrality" of his profession – just another ruse. Robert Merton's (by now) classic bourgeois position regarding the well-known and pitifully up-dated explanation of functionalist methodology is example enough of this mentality:

> Critically revised, functional analysis is neutral to the major ideological systems. To this extent, and only in this limited sense, it is like those theories and instruments of the physical sciences which lend themselves *indifferently* to use by opposed groups for purposes which are often no part of the scientist's intent.[14]
> The fact that functional analysis can be seen by some as inherently conservative and by others as inherently radical suggests that it may be inherently neither one nor the other. It suggests that functional analysis may involve no *intrinsic* ideological commitment although, like other forms of sociological analysis, it can be infused with any one of a wide range of ideological values.[15]

What is a consistent theme throughout the writings of these apologists is the incessant denial of partisan theorizing or vested interests. Since, however, it is axiomatic that when one chooses not to decide, one decides, one finds it particularly annoying to debate with someone who insists, such as Merton does above, that he hasn't taken sides. An excellent example of this kind of sheer stupidity or just plain cowardice is a recent American sociology convention. In 1967, a radical caucus proposed a resolution calling for a condemnation by the American Sociological Association of the conduct of the United States in what it called

> the government's reliance on massive and indiscriminate force to achieve its ends in Vietnam is creating a climate in which violence is used to deal with pressing domestic issues. The disparity between the enormous financial and personal resources committed to this military adventure and the meager resources devoted to the urban ghettos makes it impossible to deal effectively with the problems of poverty and race in American society. We therefore demand an immediate end to the bombing of Vietnam and the immediate withdrawal of American troops from South Vietnam.[16]

What was the response to this bold declaration and demand by the radical caucus at that convention? "The executive council's response was unequivo-

14. Robert Merton, *Social Theory and Social Structure* (New York: Free Press, 1968), p. 96.
15. *Ibid.*, p. 93.
16. J. David Colfax and Jack L. Roach, "Introduction–The Roots of Radical Sociology", *Radical Sociology* (New York: Basic Books, 1971), p. 8.

cal: 'The ASA should not, as a scientific and professional organization, express an official policy statement on political issues.'"[17] Can the Nizan book be brought up-to-date any more effectively by the executive council's response? Do you really doubt what their response would have been under the Weimar Republic?

But perhaps the philosopher, Howard L. Parsons, best describes the scope of theorizing in Western societies when he wryly remarks:

> Their [American theorists'] attention to surface rather than to depth, to individual behavior or experience rather than to social dynamics, to immediate appearance rather than underlying processes, to existing structure of personality, role and institution rather than to insurgent social transformation, to static details rather than to dissolving and developing patterns, to passive responsiveness and dependency on environment rather than to active and creative change, to individuality and other-directedness rather than to interactive and reconstructive relations of persons with other persons and with their world, to isolated "facts" rather than to facts as means to man's values – such is a symptom that theorists themselves have been determined and captured by the objects of their study and that the educators themselves need to be educated.[18]

Thus, the ideology, theories, etc., of intellectuals in any society *do*, as indicated by these Western, neutral eunuchs, reflect the ideas, goals, etc., of the ruling class. It was precisely towards one of these muddled characters that Marx directed the theme of his book, *The Poverty of Philosophy*, when he assailed P. Proudhon as a muddle-headed petty bourgeois. His words are a burning indictment of the intentions of bourgeois intellectuals:

> And this is no accident. From head to foot M. Proudhon is the philosopher and economist of the petty bourgeoisie. In an advanced society the *petty bourgeois* is necessarily from his very position a socialist on the one side and an economist on the other; that is to say he is dazed by the magnificence of the big bourgeoisie and has sympathy for the sufferings of the people. He is at once both bourgeois and man of the people. Deep down in his heart he flatters himself that he is impartial and has found the right equilibrium, which claims to be something different from mediocrity. A petty bourgeois of this type glorifies *contradiction* because contradiction is the basis of his existence. He is himself nothing but social contradiction in action. He must justify in theory what he is in practice, and M. Proudhon has the merit of being the scientific interpreter of the French petty bourgeoisie – a genuine merit, because the petty bourgeoisie will form an integral part of all the impending social revolutions.[19]

17. *Ibid.*, p. 8.
18. Howard L. Parsons, "Lenin's Theory of Personality". In Paul K. Crosser, *et al.*, *East–West Dialogues* (Amsterdam: Grüner, 1973), p. 85.
19. Karl Marx, *The Poverty of Philosophy* (4th ed.; New York: International, 1971), p. 193.

The essential point to retain is that in socialist countries, in contrast to capitalist ones, the proletariat *is* the ruling class, from whose ranks intellectuals, social scientists, artists, are obtained. Moreover, there's no inherent, long-range, profound antagonism between intellectuals and the people as there is in Western societies. Nonetheless, during the last two decades, a radically new and creative intellectual in the West, albeit with many handicaps, has been developing; in a very real sense this type of intellectual is willing to put his mental ability, education, articulateness and experience to some political or social use, in that he is not satisfied, ultimately, with merely interpreting economic, social or political events around himself, but is trying to change them.[20] (This began to occur, e.g., on a large scale, in America in the late 1960's.) He thus fuses theory and praxis, and is likely to formulate an ideology or adhere to one.

Thus, to correct Robert Merton's thesis concerning the distrust and suspicion cast upon intellectuals, only in bourgeois, capitalist countries do intellectuals dealing with human affairs find themselves in a less secure status than the physical or biological scientists. This is, in part, due to the relative indeterminacy of the social scientists' findings with respect to the proposed solutions, according to the functionalist Merton.[21] Contrary to Merton's argument, however, this indeterminacy stems from their reluctance to confront the real contradictions and conflicts of their (bourgeois) society. Indeed, this is one of the thrusts of Gouldner's new book, *The Coming Crisis of Western Sociology*, in his attack on academic sociology. Only the newly emerging radicals within all the major social and physical sciences, in their investigations and examinations of the culturally prescribed values and beliefs, discover the *non*-logical, *non*-functional, and corrupt nature of the system. Of this, Richard Hofstadter wrote:

> The voices of the political dissenters express an alienation that is at least politically meaningful, and, whatever their excesses [nihilism and anarchism], they have engaged in some kind of dialogue with and feel a responsibility to the rest of the intellectual world.[22]

Edward Shils' observation concerning the negativism of intellectuals, mentioned earlier, then, should only apply to those social structures which perpetuate and champion the interests of a tiny ruling class *over* the working class – in short, Western, bourgeois societies. This can and does, however, occur in socialist countries too, but it is not essentially *inherent* in such societies (perhaps only in their moments of deep contradiction in their devel-

20. Cf. Thomas Molnar, *The Decline of the Intellectual* (New York: Meridian Books, 1961), p. 92.
21. Cf. Merton, *op. cit.*, p. 265.
22. Richard Hofstadter, *Anti-Intellectualism in American Life* (New York: Knopf, 1963), p. 420.

opment and growth, or in their crisis-laden encounters with imperialist penetrations or aggression). Writing of such a dominant, intellectual force in the Unites States, C. W. Mills, the radical sociologist who loathed the sociological establishment in America, remarks caustically:

> As an intellectual articulation, the conservative mood is merely a reformulation of classic liberalism in the entirely unclassical age of the twentieth century; it is the image of society in which authority is at a minimum because it is guided by the autonomous forces of the magic market. The 'providence' of classic conservatism becomes liberalism's generalization of the 'unseen hand' of the market, for, in secular guise, Providence refers to a faith that the unintended consequences of many wills form a pattern, and that this pattern ought to be allowed to work itself out. Accordingly, it can be said that there is no elite, that there is no ruling class, that there are no powerful centers which need defense. Instead of justifying the power of an elite by portraying it favorably, one denies that any set of men, any class, any organization has any really consequential power. American liberalism is thus readily made to sustain the conservative mood. It is, in fact, because of the dominance of such liberal terms and assumptions that no need is felt by the elite of power and wealth for an explicitly conservative ideology.[23]

Perhaps the best known example of an *antagonistic* ruling *stratum* in a socialist society is that of the Rákosi régime in Hungary (see Herbert Aptheker's *The Truth about Hungary;* New York, Mainstream, 1957; also see Chapter III for an analysis of the Hungarian upheaval). The possibility that such an antagonistic stratum could exist, e.g., because of the various weaknesses those developing socialist societies exhibited in the dangerous Cold War encounter, seems to diminish over time, probably mainly due to economic and social advancements. In extremely trying times, times of great economic contradiction, it is more difficult for the masses to follow revolutionary, proletarian discipline, so their party representatives "make up" for that; and here *deformational* potential develops further. It is of this real and evident possibility, then, that Aptheker again wrote in his examination of the 1968 Czechoslovakian crisis:

> What were the problems inside Czechoslovakia that came to a head in 1968? Economic malfunction became a fact, ... [reforms] tended towards inflation, heavy dependence upon the West – for credits, markets and supplies – and the imposition of penalties (in addition to inflation) – even unemployment – upon sections of the working class.
> Administrative and legal abuses were numerous and severe... Promises were made [to the Soviet Union] and some positive steps were taken but the promises were greater than the deeds and the abuses were serious.

23. C. Wright Mills, *The Power Elite* (New York: Oxford University Press, 1956), p. 336.

Formal rather than real actions were frequent and aggravating. Thus, to meet the question of politically-loyal civil and state employees it was ordered that all such personnel must either join the Party or leave their positions... joining the Party, under such circumstances, and actually being Communists were in too many cases quite different things. Certain economic changes, especially in the nature of ownership and employment at service establishments, also were purely formal and often induced bitterness and deteriorated service.

The dependence upon administrative measures reflected and buttressed rigidity; all this helped produce an atmosphere which inhibited technical-scientific advances and seemed to penalize fresh thinking. Intensifying this was a certain anti-intellectualism that manifested itself, for example, in a rather crude egalitarianism with the result that scientists, technicians and physicians were grossly underpaid.

All of the above sums up to a disastrous neglect of ideology.[24]

One can find remarkable similarities between the "new Marxists" and the bourgeois intellectuals and academics, and I believe it essential to the solidarity and progress of international socialism to observe these analogous patterns. In addition, in a one-party (or communist party-led coalition), class-harmonious, socialist society, one might believe that Marxists ("orthodox") would be hard pressed to explain how such a "new opposition" develops. For how do these dissenting scholars, artists, writers, etc., come to be regarded in this case? Might not a feeling of frustration and isolation also be experienced by the new critics in these societies? Might not Shils' comment on the negativism of intellectuals be valid even here?

Stéfan Anguélov, Vice-Director of the Institute of Philosophy of the Bulgarian Academy of Sciences, denounces the revisionists as bourgeois idealists.[25] Nevertheless, the "new Marxists" consistently describe themselves as Marxist, i.e. not *opposed*, as Shils has written, to the "prevalent value system". Indeed, the words of Czech novelist and notable purveyor of revisionist nonsense, Ludvik Vaculik, during the crisis of the Dubcek fiasco, reveal the sentiment of *most* revisionists – I say most only because there are those who *are* able to change colors in the same amount of time that it takes to fly from Europe to the Pentagon building in Washington, D. C. Vaculik stated provocatively in Prague in 1967:

...With my criticism of the powers that be in this state, I have no intention of opposing socialism. I am not convinced that such a development [socialism] is necessary in our country...[26]

24. Herbert Aptheker, *Czechoslovakia and Counter-Revolution* (New York: New Outlook, 1969), pp. 15–16.
25. Cf. Stéfan Anguélov, "Reflection and Practice", in Crosser, *East–West Dialogues.*
26. Cited in Benjamin B. Page's *The Czechoslovak Reform Movement, 1963–1968* (Amsterdam: Grüner, 1973), p. 10.

In connection with the "opposition within" and with reference to Shils' ideological description, what is the significance, socially, of the intellectual unless he has freedom of expression, has influence upon the various segments of social institutions in societies, can participate in social change and receive the resulting prestige for himself, and, more importantly, for the values espoused by his society? If then, as in the Eastern European countries, society constitutes one unified force held together by both the common consciousness as well as a disciplined, democratically centralized party organization, one function of which is to clarify policies and discuss future plans of action within a Marxist-Leninist framework, either the "new intellectual" must vegetate on the fringes of the social structure or else establish working relationships with the party in command. The salience of choosing the latter course of action can only be further supported by the events in Czechoslovakia in 1968 which demonstrate the proclivity of intellectuals to regard the efforts of more disciplined and loyal intellectuals in "working out" their disagreements with the Party as, in the words of Hofstadter, "a subtle sell-out or soft corruption which forces him to lose that precious tincture of rage so necessary to first-rate creativity in a writer, that capacity for negation and rebellion that is necessary to the candid social critic, that initiative and independence of aim required for distinguished work in science".[27]

However, before turning our attention to this relationship between the powers and the intellectuals, it will be helpful to mention those groups which the intellectuals must reach with his ideas and without whose constant feedback and criticism the intellectual rapidly loses his social perspective. For the revisionist and non-revisionist alike, that common group is the *working class* as an audience. Indeed, audiences of this type serve two purposes for the intellectual: they are used as a means of justifying, in part, his ideas, perspectives, criticisms, etc., but more specifically, they are used as a measure of success, according to their (the audience's) type and size. We must keep this finding in mind when we discuss the distinct sense of isolation and frustration experienced by the Eastern European revisionist; for he does not, by and large, have widespread support for his ideas (except, of course, from the camps of the imperialist and counter-revolutionary forces who encourage at every opportunity anti-communist propaganda coming from within), and, although his audience consists of many students and fellow intellectual and institutional persons, the one audience that he really needs to maintain his status and economic position will not give him much applause. That is the audience with whom the intellectual, in order to apply himself in a non-alienative fashion, must align himself, withholds its praise, attention and support. Thus, political and social conflicts, such as the Hungarian, Polish and Czechoslovakian, ensue which, in turn, produce hostility and resent-

27. Hofstadter, *op. cit.*, p. 416.

ment of such magnitude that the dissenting intellectuals are literally forced underground or into the self-imposed isolation of the circles of gadflies whose views they share (again, for Svitak and others, this was carried to the extreme of actually defecting into the arms of working-class enemies). One analogous case can also be seen to occur in the arena of the so-called "Western Marxist", e.g. in the Frankfurt School. Here the intellectuals constitute a more clearly defined class (with specific economic class interests mentioned earlier, viz. petty bourgeois interests and status).[28] Robert Steigerwald, the West German Marxist, in attempting to explain how such *ambiguous* circles of dissent, such as the Frankfurt School, arise, writes:

> Marcuse's theory is not the whim of an individual personality, but stems from the frame of mind of an entire social stratum. It pertains to the new intellectual petty bourgeoisie, which is aware that it stands in a hopeless position historically; but it is not prepared, on the other hand, to place itself completely and without reservation at the side of the workers' socialist movement. Rather it justifies its characteristic station between the two fronts by a subtle anti-socialism. Everywhere in the work of Marcuse, Adorno, and others, tracing all the way back to Stirner, we find furious efforts to emphasize the [*ego*], and in no way yield it to a *collectivity* [my italics] that would determine it. Access to the future must be open and unlimited. Everything that exists now is equally contemptible.[29]

With these kinds of inclinations, with respect to the theory of the "new Marxists", it is entirely predictable that they would be receiving a negative evaluation, not only from most of the intellectual community, but from the official leadership of the party as well. The resulting feelings of despair and anger stemming from the rebuke produce frustrations which threaten the entire system of one's personality and security.[30] Thus Steigerwald's comment regarding the lack of commitment on the part of revisionist philosophers, etc., stemming from their specific status vis-à-vis the working class, accurately describes the "new Marxists" and should help the reader *under-*

---

28. It is also always a potential danger in socialist societies that the oppositionists' *real* aim can be their own *detachment* from the interests of the proletariat, i.e. the construction of an élite petty bourgeoisie with interests antagonistic to workers ("mere" workers), a petty bourgeois outlook imported from bourgeois intellectuals of the West. There are also *categories* or degrees of "opposition" within the East European milieux, encompassing *counter*-revolutionary opposition (whether subjective or objective, in effect) to *loyal* opposition, e.g., in the latter category (of loyal opposition–at least *over a period of time*) the case of Georg Lukács (whose theory and practice sometimes left much to be desired) comes to mind. Naturally, *critiques* of shortcomings and defects come continuously from the *non*-opposition or Party intellectuals too (*within* the Party), and it is altogether (dialectically) necessary.
29. Robert Steigerwald, "Herbert Marcuse's 'Critical Theory'". *Contemporary East European Philosophy*, IV, p. 345.
30. Cf. Robin Williams, "Propositions on Intergroup Hostility and Conflict", *Sociological Analysis*, ed. Logan Wilson (New York: Harcourt, Brace, 1949), pp. 943–946.

stand the often neurotic and disoriented behavior, such as anti-communist tirades and defections, which they display.

In view of this strained and vacillating position of the revisionists, it is not difficult to assess their measure of influence, and therefore the magnitude of their power. This can be done simply by observing the extent to which men of power follow their advice, or the extent to which these intellectuals are able to instill their own values and beliefs into the consciousness of the working populations in their countries; this, then, points to the particular role and subsequent failure of the "new Marxists": they have not managed to secure the support of any large segment of the population in their respective countries. Yet if they have influenced the Party in their countries, it has been in a negative way. For example, much of the rhetoric and anti-bureaucratic constructs developed by the "new world revisionists" has been immediately seized upon by the bourgeois press, not only to embarrass the Party in the particular country from which the revisonist operates, but to spread more vicious lies concerning the status and progress of international socialism – afterall, do not the Eastern European countries constitute, as was mentioned earlier, newly emerging models of socialist success? Aptheker, in his attempt to show the overt, counter-revolutionary atmosphere pervading Czechoslovakia before the Soviet Union intervened, cites the observations of "a university student in Los Angeles, who sent dispatches from Europe to the newsletter known as William Winter Comments (issued from Sausalito, Cal.)",[31] which should convince the reader of the seriousness with which anti-communist forces pursue the slightest hints of dissatisfaction among these socialist citizens of Eastern Europe and elsewhere:

> ...the Czechs I spoke to all insisted that they wanted a "democratic socialism". After one of the meetings I invited a Czech couple to have coffee with me. I again posed the same question as to what they wanted, and they said "75% wanted free enterprise". They wanted to be able to own their own business, and he said that as soon as the law allows it, he would go into business. The reason I posed the question to this couple is that it seemed most Czechs were parroting Dubcek in this presumed desire for "democratic socialism" and to remain in the Warsaw Pact. But that they said that in order not to upset the applecart, to give the Russians an excuse to intervene. Furthermore, *I got the feeling* [bourgeois types rarely miss an opportunity to inject this kind of poison into socialist bloodstreams], that they'll let Dubcek call it "socialism" to please the Russians as long as they can do what they want – free enterprise, or whatever [my italics].[32]

At any rate, regardless of the degree of coverage they receive from the imperialist press, the display of despair and frustration, alienation and antipathy by the revisionists clearly places them in the category of *disillusioned* or *unattached scholars*. In this status, the "new Marxists" espousing quasi-

31. Aptheker, *op. cit.*, p. 21–22.
32. *Ibid.*, p. 22.

Marxist, idealist propositons demonstrate the degree to which they have been caught up in their purely academic surroundings – this is not to gainsay the severe economic and political crises which *were* very real at the time of the disturbances, but these distortions of and mistakes against proper socialist policy ought not to be dealt with by *equally* distorted and disoriented remedies.

Thus, although intellectuals everywhere are concerned with men of power in their culture, their leaders, these "new Marxists" relate in an estranged way to the official Party men. On the one hand, their need to be active members of a political unit, a cause, etc., leads them to accept some type of authority, while on the other hand, philosophical and "humanistic" differences preclude the giving of their support to the established Party leadership. Their search for some authoritative *collectivity* to which to pledge their allegiance takes the form of an "opposition within".

The new intellectual can expect to meet with continued resistance to the particular modifications and proposals they suggest within the East European context. In Shils' opinion, this would have a tendency to produce "apathetic idiocy or regression into the acceptance of the traditional pattern of life in a society".[33] As one might *expect* who has submitted other "functionalist" theories to a radical analysis, however, this has not occurred in Eastern Europe! The various "oppositionists" are almost *super*-active, despite their heavy frustrations. Simply because the "new revisionists" have either been mildly rebuked or been given no social or political sanction, does not mean that the major means of communicating their ideas are separated from these "new Marxists", as evidenced by the numerous magazines, periodicals, and seminars operated by them. And, of course, these dissenters are constant sources of criticism used by the imperialist and reactionary elements in the Western world – which can only be verified by the rapid publishing by the bourgeois press of *any* of the writings of the "new Marxists".

Nonetheless, the "opposition within" has essentially not been very successful in defining their role according to the particular conditions of their respective countries. They also fail to comprehend the significance of their theory and practice in terms of international implications for the socialist cause. As Steigerwald above noted, their political affiliation or opposition has not been decided on the basis of a conscious orientation in society nor in accordance with the demands of intellectual life for revolutionaries. Further, Mannheim sketches the intellectual, sociological problem for revisionists in the following passage from *Ideology and Utopia*:

> Every political figure operating at this level of consciousness [a course of action which "proceeds by attempting to comprehend the theories and their mutations

33. Edward Shils, "The Intellectuals in the Political Development of the New States". *World Politics*, vol. 12, April, 1960, p. 344.

in close relation to the collective groups and typical total situations out of which they arose and whose exponents they are. The inner connections between thought and social existence must in this case be reconstructed. It is not 'consciousness in itself' which arbitrarily chooses from several possible alternatives, nor does the single individual construct an *ad hoc* theory to suit the needs of a given single situation; but it is rather that social groups having a certain type of structure formulate theories corresponding to their interests as perceived by them in certain situations. As a result, for each specific social situation there are discovered certain modes of thinking and possibilities of orientation"][34] which is appropriate to our present stage of intellectual development thinks – implicitly, if not explicitly – in terms of structural situations. This type of thinking alone gives meaning and concreteness to action oriented to some far-off goal, though momentary decisions may well rest on momentary orientations. Thus, he is protected against empty and schematic generalities and is at the same time given sufficient flexibility so that he will not be overimpressed by some single event of the past as an inadequate model for future action.

The man who is purposefully active will never ask how some revered leader acted in a past situation, but rather how he would really orient himself to the present situation. This ability to reorient oneself anew to an ever newly forming constellation of factors constitutes the essential practical capacity of the type of mind which is constantly seeking orientation for action.

In the exposition of political interrelationships, the purely contemplative attitude must never be allowed to displace the original need of the political person for active orientation.[35]

Let the "opposition within" contemplate those words!

(b) *Some Dialectics of "Opposition".*

Whenever Lenin spoke of the role of the intellectual in socialist movements, he invariably linked it to the function of the Party, to organization, to discipline. As one scholar of Leninism, Alfred Meyer, explains:

> The party is ... to be composed of those intellectuals, *whatever their background*, who have acquired consciousness and, prompted by ideas and convictions, have turned into revolutionaries by profession, men [as a party] whose vocation it is... "to make the proletariat capable of fulfilling its great historical mission" [quotation from Lenin].[36]

Lenin's description of the duties and functions of the revolutionary intellectual can be applied in both prerevolutionary, capitalist society as well as in countries in which a revolution has been accomplished. What is the dialectic which traces the emergence of the intellectual as an apologist of the status quo into its destroyer? We turn again to Meyer, who observes:

34. Mannheim, *Ideology and Utopia* (New York: Harcourt, Brace, 1968), pp. 156–157.
35. *Ibid.*, p. 157.
36. Alfred G. Meyer, *Leninism* (New York: Praeger, 1967), p. 33. My italics.

According to Leninism, the carriers of proletarian class consciousness were bourgeois intellectuals, whose consciousness is the product of the dialectics of ideas. They become conscious by carrying the heritage of liberal thought to its logical conclusion. Intellectuals, thought Lenin, were members of the bourgeois or gentry who had been declassed and uprooted by acquiring an education. Ideas were at work in their heads and were turning their thoughts toward social criticism. They mirrored the ills of their society, and the socialist ideas held by bourgeois intellectuals could only be understood by knowing the capitalist society they criticized and wanted to abolish.[37]

Of course, Lenin knew that the majority of intellectuals served mainly as ideological spokesmen for the ruling classes; and, since Marxist-Leninists work for the "dictatorship of the proletariat" in society, it necessarily follows that the intellectuals in such societies are, if not servants, then promoters of the workers' causes. Thus, in this sense, the functions of the intellectual in capitalist societies, as stated by Lenin, are similar to the functions of the intellectual working in socialist environments, with at least one major difference. In the latter case, social reality and conditions are more clearly and correctly observed, i.e. social relationships and social structures are identified and scientifically analyzed to promote *deeper understanding* of reality; rather than just a prop for exploitive power, the intellectual works so that the workers' power can be *enlarged*. The role of ideologue for the exploiter is replaced by the role of the rational and humanistic planner within the proletarian organization. There is, then, an enormous restructuring in the *telos* of the intellectual, hence in interests and consciousness.

If there are serious theoretical and practical differences between the "new revisionists" and the "orthodox" Marxists, then there emerges a dilemma for world revolutionaries vis-à-vis the class struggle; for as Lenin points out decisively:

Since there can be no talk of an independent ideology formulated by the working masses themselves in the process of their movement, the *only* choice is either bourgeois or socialist ideology. There is no middle course (for mankind has not created a "third" ideology, and, moreover, in a society torn by class antagonisms there can never be a non-class or an above-class ideology).[38]

If Marxist-Leninists are to take the above quote from Lenin's work to be historically valid, then the Eastern European revisionists must tend to

37. *Ibid.*, pp. 31–32. The social scientist, Lenski, puts this much less dialectically, when he states: "...Intellectuals are likely to be the leaders of social revolution. They alone can supply the one crucial ingredient without which social revolutions are impossible – a new ideology to challenge and destroy the existing one. Ideologies are the stock in trade of intellectuals. They are the opinion leaders with respect to important philosophical questions. Intellectuals are easily alienated by systems of power and privilege. They are like ministers without portfolio, experts without the power to translate their ideas into public policy." Gerhard Lenski, *Power and Privilege* (New York: McGraw-Hill, 1966), p. 70.
38. V. I. Lenin, *What Is to Be Done? Collected Works* (Moscow, 1961), vol. 5, p. 384.

become congruent with their Western analogues, both ideologically and practically, unless they demonstrate very clearly their class alignments as being consistent with the teachings of Marx, Engels, *and* Lenin. For it is the tendency of the revisionists to place themselves *above* the political, economic and social situations in their respective countries, to classify themselves as "independent" Marxists, more critical in their thinking; that has, as mentioned earlier, disoriented them to the extent that they no longer respect organized, working party channels; as a result, their demands are as unrealistic as are their theoretical bases. In a limited sense, they resemble the "new American middle-class anarchists" who consider themselves the only *truly* revolutionary group in sight.

Attempting to account for the presumed general propensity of the intellectuals to be "leftist" in both East and West, Helmut Plessner, a critic of Marxism, relates a general connection between the exact sciences and a leaning toward left-wing ideas:

> For those engaged in the exact sciences, where ideas are mainly framed in a mathematical form, and where the progress of knowledge is based on controlled experiments and on the difficult application of theoretical results to objective experience, there is a strong attraction in the doctrines of enlightened positivism. The clearest expression of this type of approach in the spheres of political ideology is to be found in the doctrines of Marxism [sic]. The close connection established by Marx between the exact sciences and the technique of industry on the one hand, and the structure of political power on the other, has a special appeal for the scientist who sees in it the key to the truly rational world community of the future.[39]

Plessner, of course, in this contention, has much difficulty producing evidence of Marxism's popularity *predominantly* among members of the physical sciences in the United States; it is common knowledge that the majority of the radical students espousing one form or another of Marxism during the last ten years in the United States have overwhelmingly been working in fields such as psychology, sociology, political science, philosophy, and related disciplines within the *social* sciences. This is not to deny any scientific base for these social sciences; but the two, physical sciences and social sciences, can hardly be fully equated, thus weakening Plessner's argument. This is also not to deny the solidly scientific basis of Marxism-Leninism but rather to establish the universal appeal of Marxism to physical and social scientist alike. Thus, Plessner's hypothesis does not shed much light on the general proclivites of the "independent Marxists" in both the East and West with respect to their often juvenile, suicidal demands for absolute freedom, nor does it help anyone in determining the actual reasons why men choose Marxism over other doctrines.

39. Cited by Seymour Martin Lipset, *Political Man* (New York: Doubleday, 1963), p. 343.

Leszek Kolakowski, however, a revisionist himself, provides us with an explanation of a common problem for left-intellectuals, both East and West:

> In capitalist countries, the left struggles against the limitations of freedom of speech and expression. It does also in non-capitalist lands. In one and the other the left fights all the contradictions of freedom that arise in *both kinds* of social conditions. How far can one push the demand for tolerance without turning against the idea of tolerance itself? How can one guarantee that tolerance will not lead to the victory of forces that will strangle the principle of tolerance? This is the great problem of all leftist movements.[40]

One has already experienced the dangerous drift of sanction mentioned by Kolakowski above in the events surrounding both the Hungarian and Czechoslovakian incidents. If one might judge from these examples the extent to which the "left" has handled their "problem", one would be forced to conclude that the emperor has no clothes. The "problem" that Kolakowski refers to, then, was one faced by Lenin and his revolutionary forces; Lenin's solution was to *strengthen* Party discipline and to *eliminate* most of the counter-revolutionary forces. To those revisionists seeking "freedom", one is prompted to ask them: At what price? In terms, then, of strengthening Party discipline, do the revisionists seriously doubt that today's international economic and political imperialism is strong enough to take advantage of their "demands for increased freedom in the form of multi-parties, publications, etc.," so that the newly-won gains under socialism's banner might all be lost to Ivan Svitak's Columbia gang? If that's the price, the Party is not paying!

But if the East European revisionist, in spite of his basic anti-Party stance and myriad reform proposals, is able to maintain, nonetheless, his position, status and activities (except when the Party feels that disaster is imminent), the same does not hold true for the Western intellectual whether he aligns himself with the establishment or whether he insists upon a detached relationship. Thus, American or Western scholars perceive themselves as a rather marginal group, deprived of the proper social recognition, proportionate income, and power. Indeed, with few exceptions (Henry Kissinger, Daniel P. Moynihan, Arthur Schlesinger, to name a few) intellectuals do not even deserve the status of advisor to the power groups in the United States. One aspect of this American phenomenon (which can be seen to be used somewhat apologetically by the bourgeois theorist) is suggested by Lipset:

> ...His [the American intellectual's] feelings of inferiority derive from his glorified concept of the European intellectual's status, and from using the European situation as a point of reference and comparison. ...It is certainly true that there is a difference between the European and the American treatment of the intellectual. The difference is no more than the difference between a fairly rigid class

---

40. Leszek Kolakowski, "The Concept of the Left", *Essential Works of Socialism*, ed. Irving Howe (New York: Bantam, 1970), p. 691.

society and a society which emphasizes equality. In Europe, open deference is given to all those with higher status, whether engineers, factory owners or professors, while in the United States, it is not given to any degree that it is given abroad.[41]

Lipset would have us believe, just as he does with respect to social mobility in the U. S., that it is the enduring American belief in egalitarianism which sharply differentiates American society and its intellectuals from the more status-oriented cultures of Europe. In general, Europe has known classes defined by heredity, or otherwise sharply or permanently determined in composition and social status, which have had a stake in defending the status quo.

This very significant distinction, according to Lipset, does not demonstrate any noticeable trends of anti-intellectualism, but, on the contrary, as Lipset continues:

...An American worker will show as little deference to the engineer who tries to tell him how to run his machine as his son will toward his professor. One study of the relative prestige of different occupations showed that a random sample of the American population ranked college professors higher in status than other professions or businessmen...

...[This] challenges the common impression of many observers, and of the American intellectuals themselves, that the status of intellectuals in the society is low. Indeed, this contrast between the self-image of the intellectuals and the fact that they are held in high esteem by the public at large illustrates the disparity between American equalitarianism and European status-orientation.[42]

Contrary to Lipset's *abstract* interpretation of intellectuals in America, one can point to both Richard Hofstadter's *Anti-Intellectualism in American Life* and the McCarthy Era as much more indicative of the *precarious* position in which American scholars find themselves (as opposed to the milieu of contemporary Eastern European Marxists who, in many cases, often make top-level political decisions and are popular and accessible to the working population, as has been reported by Carey),[43] notwithstanding all the references to "equalitarianism". Hofstadter in a more appropriate vein writes:

It appears, then, to be the fate of intellectuals either to berate their exclusion from wealth, success, and reputation, or to be seized by guilt [and justly so] when they overcome this exclusion. They are troubled, for example, when power

41. Lipset, *Political Man*, p. 352.
42. Seymour Martin Lipset and Reinhard Bendix, *Social Mobility in Industrial Society* (Berkeley: University of California Press, 1959), p. 111. It may also show that the pro-intellectual propaganda of the Eisenhower administration in its struggle to contend scientifically with the U.S.S.R. (Sputnik, etc.) was successful at that point. A similar study might not show this now (1972) especially in view of the major cutbacks (40% during the first four years of Nixon's régime) in Federal aid to education in recent times. Where would that leave Lipset's "equalitarian" hypothesis?
43. Cf. William Carey, *New Man or No Man* (New Bearings, 1969), pp. 134–135.

disregards the counsels of intellect, but because they fear corruption they are even more troubled when power comes to intellect for counsel. To revert to Professor Howe's language: bourgeois society rejects them, that is only one more proof of its philistinism; when it gives them an "honored place", it is buying them off. The intellectual is either shut out or sold out.[44]

It should be borne in mind that some Western theorists have suggested, also, that, although the Eastern European scholars, in general, are accorded a higher status and given a lager role in power-politics, only the high officers in the Communist Parties of Eastern Europe can confer nominations on Party intellectuals. In this way, such critics argue that the various Parties reward only those intellectuals who maintain the Party line, by giving them enviable sinecures at various libraries, universities, and publishing houses, by granting high royalties, by providing large apartments and weekend houses, and even by facilitating trips abroad. As socialist economies expand, however, such a criticism loses its concreteness, since by now writers' unions, staffs of institutes, professors, as well as workers, have collectively reached a stage where these institutions themselves supply jobs, apartments, bonuses, weekend and summer houses, and trips abroad. But earlier, the struggle against such unfair eventualities by communist parties can be discerned in János Kádár's speech of 1957 (immediately following the unsuccessful counter-revolution of 1956, in Hungary). Kádár forcefully sets forth the relationship between the Communist Party members and non-Party people. He states:

Difficult though it may be, communists will have to accept the principle that, in the eyes of the law, party members have not an iota more right than do non-party people. We must fight to assert this principle; and if it should be found that some people joined the party because they thought that membership would entail more rights for them, then steps should be taken to discourage such people from party membership. What distinguishes party members from non-party people is quite another thing – it is the fact that members of the party work in a proper and exemplary way. A communist who does good work enjoys such respect and prestige in the party committee or branch organization that no office whatever could give him that much. All members of the party will have to put up with the fact that they are granted no more civic rights than non-party people.[45]

Uninspired by the class struggle, however, the vocal dissenters of Eastern Europe, like their Western radical "counterparts", provide themselves with a central theme, on which they hope to build a larger movement capable of exerting greater pressure on Communist Party leaders. In addition, they are

44. Hofstadter, op. cit., p. 417.
45. János Kádár, "Challenge and Crisis in the Hungarian Communist Party", in Communist Political Systems, ed. Alvin Z. Rubinstein (Prentice-Hall, 1966), p. 146.

about as conscious as their American, "pluralistic", *non-aligned* cohorts (both groups reflecting an extremely non-sociological conception of the mechanisms by which societies transmit and maintain themselves) of what Barrows Dunham refers to as "the anarchy of opinion" – too much dissent and not enough unity.[46] Communist Party members have insisted that, in spite of the anarchistic ravings of the "new revisionists", social ties, historical traits, etc., must not be attempted to be *totally* or *immediately* destroyed; that, although one must work to raise the consciousness of workers and others, to the extent that the goals and values of socialism are to be embraced, one cannot do that by waving the wand of some celestial historical negation. In short, tradition dies hard, and in the meantime transitional periods must be expected. This approach has allowed periodic pockets of resistance (sometimes reaching crescendo proportions) to and reaction against the existing Party programs. Thus, nationalistic fervor, religious bigotry, resistance to collectivization, etc., have induced the Party to assert its role strongly, from time to time, in the planning of socialist societies; although frequently in the history of the Eastern European countries, Party leaders have tolerated, in varying degrees, these traditionally supported tendencies, hoping that future gains made under the banner of socialism and its programs would negate their influence. Of course, as history shows, bourgeois exploiters and reactionaries have used this atmosphere of tolerance and indulgence in their attempts to reverse the progress of socialism in these countries– and when the Party recognizes this drift (as especially in the Czechoslovakian case, 1968), and employs its power to prevent such counter-revolutionary activities, cries of dogmatism and repression are heard from the mouths of those "new Marxists" either perilously unaware or foolishly ignorant of the revanchists among them.

During periods of crisis, when the Party attempts to offset the impact of "internal opposition", e.g. by official censorship, a member of the "opposition within", because of his socially and politically unacceptable views, is likely to be regarded as a marginal person with whom it is considered inadvisable to associate. A feeling of futility in these theorists results, as the Party attempts to keep their influence to a minimum. In Hungary, e.g., Georg Lukács was removed from all official positions (because of his participation in the ill-fated Nagy régime) as well as *numerous* disciples scattered about in non-teaching institutes – all of these also being dropped from Party membership (or resigning). DeGrood explains some of the recent historical circumstances surrounding Lukács:

The Hungarian Party had categorized Lukács' thought as a species of revisionism, and therefore not only was Lukács unable to teach but also many of his students, some of whom resigned from the Party after the events of the Hunga-

46. Barrows Dunham, *Giant in Chains* (Boston: Little, Brown, 1953), p. 251.

rian revolt. Nevertheless, Lukács, who died this year [1971]... was readmitted [a few years ago] to the Party and disciples continue to hold posts in various important institutes in Budapest. These developments themselves attest to the liberalized atmosphere in Hungary and the growing success of the economic reforms established by the Party.[47]

Although less well-known in the West, Lukács' work was sometimes used by reactionary or revisionist writers or movements as propaganda against emerging socialist states. Lukács himself despised and rejected such a spurious use.

Moreover, when Party leaders have negatively reinforced the circulation and promotion of revisionist ideas, the dissenting intellectual is less likely to obtain the approval or respect of his peers or members of his community. This may account for the intense feelings of alienation expressed by many revisionist thinkers. Often, revisionists of a "mild" variety will go further towards anti-communism, because increasing recognition and "hero worship" of them in the West will be forthcoming. Also, the increased mobility for travel throughout the world brings about greater contact with both bourgeois and "radical" Westerners, and this helps to evolve an international "third way", without, however, setting up a real, *mass base* for such a movement – and this contradiction pushes such an intellectual further into ever more intense (and higher level) alienation. If the past is any indication, then, of the success or failure of the revisionist movement in Eastern Europe, there is much that demonstrates that the alienation, frustration, and despair felt by these "real" Marxists will increase if they persist in their present analysis.

The focal point of the spread of revisionist ideas exists in the comparative political vacuum of Yugoslavia, a country precariously perched between East and West. The Yugoslavian magazines, *Praxis* and *Gledista*, and the Korcula Summer School, gather around themselves some of the most well-known "new Marxists" (as well as various Marxist-Leninists, too); and, since the work of this Yugoslavian group is of immediate import to East European intellectuals elsewhere, the ideological struggle against revisionism by Marxist-Leninists often takes the form of an attack on those Yugoslavian intellectuals. To Gus Hall, this struggle must be won by the workers, the Party and the programs of socialism because

Revisionism prepares the soil for counter-revolution. Revisionism is the softening up process. It destroys revolutionary vigilance. It creates the confusion and the divisions that are necessary for counter-revolution.[48]

47. David H. DeGrood, "The 'Movement' at Present: Revolutionary Pause and Counter-Revolutionary Upsurge", unpublished MS. The unbelievably deep roots of Lukács' thought in Hungary is a function of at least two things: the relatively small size of the country and the tremendous (often, of course, incorrect, as admitted by Lukács himself!) theoretical depth and breadth of Lukács' philosophy.
48. Gus Hall, *Imperialism Today* (New York: International, 1972), p. 341.

Unlike their American counterpart "radicals", who can orientate themselves and sympathize with the "Third World", the Eastern European "new Marxists" can embrace neither the capitalist world nor the "Soviet-style" political compositions (and only a rare few can align themselves with the "Third World", due to the proximity, spatially and temporally, of armed forces and missiles of both antagonistic camps).

The prospects of successful praxis by the revisionists appear dark: they can neither muster the necessary support to spread their idealism, nor can they refute the advancing standard of living mentioned earlier of the countries in which they live. If anything else, precisely these socialist successes may well *add* hope to them that their own "model" of socialism, if applied, would result in a successful qualitative leap for those same countries! Perhaps some manner can be conceived and instituted, if this be true, by the official Parties to absorb their enthusiasm and devotion to various causes, while negating the defeatist opposition they pose; and perhaps not. At any rate, Marxists must be aware of the contradictions implicit in *any* path of development.

Chapter III

EASTERN EUROPEAN REVISIONISM

(a) *The Evolution of the "Opposition Within"*.

Essentially, to speak of the resurgence of revisionist Marxism in the 1950's and 1960's, one must divide the problem into at least two main areas: the historical, social, political and economic conditions which characterized Post-War Eastern Europe as well as the Soviet Union to include policies, procedures and affairs of the newly emerging socialist states across Eastern Europe; and the variegated, hostile responses and reactions to these conditions to include both those actions taken by western imperialist powers as well as the numerous reactions of Marxist philosophers, scientists, artists, etc. In order, then, to present a coherent, critical analysis of their (the revisionists') responses, in the forms of writings, behavior, and consciousness, it will first be necessary to examine the first half of the problem.

In discussing the problems confronted by two of the Eastern European countries since the end of World War II, Hungary and Poland, I hope to generalize from their experiences, approaches, and solutions, to the problems etc., facing the international socialist movement; for many of the problems which beset these Eastern European fledglings will also confront future socialist structures in countries now dominated directly or indirectly, by monopoly capital's ruling classes.

Throughout the remainder of this book I will assume, as a major underlying condition leading to or influencing both the situations of Post-War East Europe and the responses to those situations, i.e. revisionist and counter-revolutionary outbreaks, the persistent, pernicious, "machinations and pressures of the western imperialist powers", the most obvious of which is the United States. Therefore, when I speak of the errors, shortcomings, and recalcitrance in the early history of these Eastern European states, I view these acts as having been performed on the stage of western, imperialist sabotage, counter-revolutionary attempts and cold-war diplomacy – in short, anti-communist propaganda in word and deed.

Thus, with the background and social forces clearly established, the reasons for such virulent and violent actions typical of the age of resurging revisionism must be presented and discussed. In his brilliant critical study of the 1956 Hungarian uprising, *The Truth About Hungary*, Herbert Aptheker enumerates four basic sources responsible for the upheavals which shook the East European states, in particular, Hungary, which we shall deal with in depth later:

> The errors seem to have fallen into four main categories, all interrelated and rein-forcing each other. These were: 1. a failure to properly evaluate the national feelings of the Hungarian people; 2. persistence in a badly one-sided economic policy resulting in a halt to the improvements of the material conditions of the masses, and for certain periods, a decline in such conditions which never, at any time, has exceeded rather limited standards; 3. an insistence upon mono-lithic unity in all spheres of life, enforced with terrible rigidity, deteriorating into crass administrative bullying and intolerable violations of legality, humanity and sheer decency: 4. a failure to preserve the revolutionary elan and purity of the Marxist-Leninist party.[1]

In this book, written by one of the leading officials in the Communist Party of the United States, is honest, scholarly and critical proof of the self-criti-cizing potential that typifies the Communist Party and its historical role; further, Aptheker's book as well as the numerous others dedicated to the same type of integrity of analysis and truthfulness, are, by themselves, ade-quate refutation of the claims by revisionists that the Communist Parties can never change or don't desire change. But let us discuss the errors as suggested by Aptheker.

He cites the lack of understanding that Communist Party officials and Party bureaucrats brought to the Post-War Eastern European countries in terms of the deep-rooted feelings of nationalism and its related sentiments which prevailed then and, to a lesser degree, even today. For the most part, careless and overzealous Party functionaries ignored or suppressed such sentiments to such an extent that a grass-roots based opposition began to form. This opposition was fostered primarily by the former feudalist rulers, the clergy (always a bulwark of reaction and regression in East Europe), and many of the middle classes, all of course aided and abetted by the CIA and other devious sources of counter-revolution; much as appeals to patriot-ism and racism are made by the ruling circles in the Unites States to exploit existing divisions between members of the working classes and other groups in order that those élites can maintain their power, the reactionary forces in Eastern Europe effectively used the historically potent sentiments of their respective countries, in this case, to attempt to regain power and authority lost when socialism annihilated the forces of the Third Reich. However, as Aptheker rightly points out, regardless of the intentions of the reactionary forces, etc., Party officials should not have been so clumsy and offensive in their treatment of the varied forms of nationalism, as they manifested them-

1. Herbert Aptheker, *The Truth About Hungary* (New York: Mainstream Publishers, 1957), p. 134.

selves after World War II. Aptheker's historical perspective of the period, however, shows his understanding of the world situation. He writes:

> ...I think, that Communist theory classically tended to underplay the significance of national feelings and rather one-sidedly pictured patriotism as the tool of exploiters and the deceiver of the exploited. This emphasis was perfectly understandable – and even proper – when imperialism ruled the entire world and its wars were plunder campaigns camouflaged with 'patriotic' appeals.[2]
> There was a lag, in the world-wide proletarian movement, in adjusting to this change; a lag reinforced by the fundamental need for support of the Soviet Union in face of the acute danger of fascism and war; a lag especially painful as the rise of colonial and liberation movements throughout the world gave unprecedented impetus to national feelings everywhere.[3]

Compounding these errors, which limited the level of consciousness that Eastern European citizens could bring to their situation, was an *over*emphasis on establishing a solid, heavy industrial base with a corresponding lack of emphasis upon light industry or consumer production such as housing, food, clothing etc.[4] Aptheker does not intend (nor do I) to question the very basic historical and economic necessity of industrializing as quickly as possible according to socialist principles, rather, the particular route taken and procedures used are held in question. The particular shortages mentioned above, stemming from the basic policy of too rapid an industrialization process, were effectively capitalized upon by the counter-revolutionary forces whose military and economic bases existed side-by-side with the socialist states. West Berlin, for example, a lavishly subsidized and strategically utilized base contiguous to East Berlin, was intentionally made to look glamorous to the hard-pressed East Germans whose historical conditions and economic progress were, by comparison, much less favorable. Both the Soviet Union and the Eastern European states suffered enormous losses of life and property; and thus, the kind of assistance provided to West Berlin by a comfortable United States was not forthcoming immediately from the Soviet Union.

In addition to the above mentioned nearly Sisyphean entanglements, pervasive and persistent strains of nationalism and misguided or misdirected economic policies, the Eastern European states cultivated and nurtured an extremely rigid bureaucracy with the corresponding characteristics of harshness, mistrust, abuses, censorship, purges, etc., which took as their supreme model, the then Stalinist approach to controlling the Communist Party. It was against the constant imposition of censorship and reprisals, restrictions upon the consideration of criticisms and new ideas, etc., that the "New

2. *Ibid.*, p. 135.
3. *Ibid.*, p. 135. The Vietnam War may also have had a similar effect on the Czechoslovak situation.
4. Cf. *ibid.*, p. 138.

Marxists" originally began to voice their opposition. Aptheker describes both the censorship and the political terror:

> After the large-scale removal and replacement of fascist volumes, and once again beginning towards the end of 1949, there started a process of placing on special reserve or confining for special use other books, or even removing books for warehouse storage. Indeed, by about 1952 as many books were on restricted or confined or special reserves or in storage as were on the shelves for readers. It reached a point where Freud, Proudhon, Edward Bernstein, Jung, Gide, Malraux, Maurois, were unobtainable or available only after hard and courageous effort. Some musical scores were banned, some Hungarian literary classics restricted, classical works on political economy (like Adam Smith) and philosophy and history were confined to very limited circulation.[5]
>
> Beginning with the arrest and frame-up and execution of the Communist leader László Rajk, several thousand people, mostly Communists and Socialists, were more or less arbitrarily apprehended, more or less unjustly convicted, and in scores of cases – perhaps some hundreds of cases – wrongly executed. It appears also indubitable that forms of torture were used, not rarely, for purposes of extracting 'confessions' or as sheer punishment.
>
> Here, again, under capitalist rule, especially in its racist and fascist and colonial expressions, and generally in terms of the radical and the poor (and notably in pre-1945 Hungary), injustice and frame-up, police beatings, third degree tortures are institutionalized matters, known to all with any political sophistication. But their appearance, to any degree and in any form, in Socialist countries is intolerable and utterly unjustifiable – no matter what the provocation or the danger or the background. Again, too, it is exactly because such inhumanity is alien and hostile to Socialism that it aroused the popular hatred for its servants that it did arouse.[6]

The specific development of an opposition within will be discussed shortly, but the essential point to remember is that intellectual opposition to the mismanagement and perversion of the Eastern European socialist countries did not really solidify until the issues of censorship and suppression of ideas surfaced – that is until the tumultuous, harsh realities of the mistaken domestic policies hit home – in the universities and intellectual circles.

Finally, we must deal with the widespread phenomenon of either ignoring or crudely altering the historical and revolutionary role of the Communist Party, which only further heightened the controversy over censorship and restrictions. Since the Communist parties of Eastern Europe became the formal mechanisms by which the distortions of socialist principles and policies were enforced, it was understandable that the "new Marxists" were so eager to either radically reduce the power of the Party or to introduce competing parties or a multi-party system to check its power. The depths of

5. *Ibid.*, p. 150.
6. *Ibid.*, p. 150.

despair over the political executions, terror and torture conducted by the Party were all too real to the revisionists as well as other elements of the population. This despair produced, later, extremely radical and dangerous proposals as to the corrective measures necessary to prevent future misdirection and perversions. Again, Aptheker comments on this tendency toward disillusionment when he writes of the abuses:

> To such depths could Party leaders fall when their loyalty degenerated to fanaticism; when rigidity and centralization and bureaucracy had blinded them; when separation from the masses had led to cynicism and a dependence upon force; when they forgot *the* reason for the Party, for Communism – the liberation of the oppressed and, therefore, of all mankind.[7]

Thus, the underlying sources for popular discontent having been briefly examined, it is now time to investigate the particular currents along which the revisionist thinking moved in response to these errors and distortions. It is my intention to demonstrate that, although the deep dissatisfaction with the social orders of their respective countries was by itself valid enough, their persistent and reactionary responses to these grave mistakes, with a few exceptions, not only cannot be justified, but constitute potential counter-revolutionary trends within the East European front. With this orientation in mind, we can proceed to the specific "oppositions within" in the two countries mentioned earlier, Hungary and Poland.

(b) *Socialism at Stake*

The rather modest beginnings of modern revisionism center around an expected reaction of people in Eastern European countries to the arduous and overbearing rule of Joseph Stalin. This reaction and subsequent violent opposition did not occur simultaneously in these countries, but both phenomena were nurtured by those historical forces mentioned earlier. Many intellectuals and students in universities and scholars in institutes in these Eastern European countries collectively served as the catalysts for dissent. Such professors, initially in Poland, were thus opening up a vast discussion, which afterward spread to artists, writers, and to the entire intelligentsia, and through them to the Party.[8]

But this process was no historical deviation. The resistance of the intellectuals, and through them of the students at European universities, to government policy has been a significant, characteristic feature of political life in Europe since the 19th century. The universities, the professors, and the students formed a political complex which was the prime source of the "opposition within". Although not always united on either principles or strategies,

7. *Ibid.*, p. 153.
8. Cf. Ghita Ionescu, *The Politics of the European Communist States* (New York: Praeger, 1967), pp. 205–206.

not even within countries, this complex has traditionally represented a vanguard of political opposition, which took grave risks in the political units
established under Stalin and the allies of the U.S.S.R.: in Berlin in 1953, in
Poland in 1955–56, in Hungary in 1956, etc.

Let us briefly review the origin and development of the "new Marxist"
opposition of the two key countries, Poland and Hungary, the former representing a higher degree of success for revisionist elements than the latter.
For instance, in the less publicized case of Poland, the interconnected relations between the professors, the students, and the universities, and the more
dramatic political movements which they initiated, led to the formation of a
vocal and sizable minority expressing itself around the exceedingly successful *Po Prostu*, a student publication.[9] In both explosions various intellectuals were the divisive and aggravating agents, setting the foundation, stance
(once the objective conditions presented themselves), solidarity, and cohe-
siveness of Eastern European revisionism.

We turn first to Poland. According to Alicja Iwanski:

> The intelligentsia [of Poland before communism] retained the aristocratic notion
> of [the] inferiority of economic pursuits and an outward contempt for monetary
> matters; related to this was [a] disregard for all types of utilitarian activities,
> including technology and applied science.[10]

Being a distinct élite within the Polish social structure prior to 1944, the
intelligentsia was historically careful to define politics as the only variable in
their country, lest they be removed from their high position. This definition
was consistent with their contempt for both manual work and business
enterprises. Thus, Rawin explains the paradoxical dialectic which led these
feudalistic intellectuals, nevertheless, to socialism:

> Historically, ...[the Polish élite intellectuals were] either indifferent or had a
> negative attitude towards industrialism and economic modernization. This was
> associated with the conservative bent in the intelligentsia value system, and with
> the view of economic activities as a low-status function, assigned to the inferior
> strata. However, whenever confronted with the secular pressure of modern
> industrialism, the intelligentsia tended to opt for the Socialist (not necessarily
> Marxist), rather than for the capitalist solution. The determining factor in this
> choice was the anti-entrepreneurial bias inherent in the intelligentsia ideology.
> Related to this were the elitist perspective of social organization, inherited from
> gentry society, and the authoritarian concept of polity – both of which enhanced
> the compatibility between the intelligentsia outlook and the Socialist order.[11]

9. Cf. Lewis Coser, *Men of Ideas* (New York: Free Press, 1965), p. 199.
10. Cited by Solomon John Rawin, "The Polish Intelligentsia and the Socialist Order:
Elements of Ideological Compatibility". *Political Science Quarterly*, LXXIII (September
1968), pp. 356–357.
11. *Ibid.*, p. 354.

In relationship to the Communist Party, the intelligentsia were at first very much opposed to the tightly disciplined and anti-élitist ideology originating from it. From the viewpoint of the Communist Party leaders, the Polish intelligentsia appeared as a bad risk, an unnecessary burden, in fact, a bourgeois remnant.

Since part of the intelligentsia was to be the foundation for anti-Soviet activities and propaganda, and since it was concerned with maintaining its élitist structure, it could expect a response from Party leaders. The primary aim of the new Communist Party was to profoundly alter the arrangements of the institutions which supported the intelligentsia.

Confounding both the Soviet and Polish communists, opposition to such reforms came, not only from the intelligentsia, which was attempting to re-establish its supremacy as a vital élite and hold fast to its distinctive status, but also from public opinion and labor. That formerly low status individuals without proper education could be placed in positions of control and in charge of people with high status appeared incompatible with the "proper" order of things. Thus, the projected nature of the new communist order was sharply at odds with one element of the dominant value system in Poland, which thereby weakened its control over the Polish intelligentsia and other classes, an inauspicious beginning to say the least. Even so, the Polish intelligentsia were upset with the newly established communist system for much less justified reasons than the workers who, afterall, were not historically anti-communist.[12] This ideological dispute, however, does seem to verify the contention that Communist Party leaders failed to consider the particular historical and nationalist traditions intrinsic to both Poland and Hungary.

Not until 1956 did the leaders of the Communist Party there begin to fully comprehend the unique nature of the Polish situation, which, in part, helped to prevent cooperation of both Communist and non-Communist elements within the social and economic structure. At that time, Wladyslaw Gomulka (who recently was forced to resign by the pressure of workers and the Polish Communist Party), who gained power in 1956, gave the Polish people hope that new forms of governing apparatus, more compatible with the *national* tradition and free from the stigma of complete congruency with Soviet models, were to be instituted. Brought to this position of power, Gomulka was able to appeal to the nation's sense of solidarity and to legitimize his government to the extent that the barriers between the intelligentsia and his Party were dissolved. In fact, however, what occured initially was an accommodation of the intellectuals by the Gomulka government. Thus, six months later, upon analyzing the activities of those dissident groups opposed to Communist Party power and responding to criticisms of repression

12. Cf. *ibid.*, pp. 358–359.

and dogmatism, Gomulka addressed himself to those rebellious Party members and others, who were very clearly taking advantage of a relaxed atmosphere to generate sentiment for the "good old days": "If a Party member disagrees with Party policy; if he does not submit to the Party majority on questions of principle, ... if his world view prevents him from accepting the Party's ideological principle, either he leaves the ranks, gives up his Party card, or the Party must expel him."[13] Thus was the struggle between the main ideological spokesmen of the Communist Party in Poland and the revisionists born. The revisionists, in this case, were as Coser puts it, the "quite heterogeneous group of Polish intellectuals within the Communist Party and around its fringes, who, in 1955, had begun to waken from their dogmatic slumbers and had become the ideological spokesmen for the October Revolution of 1956".[14]

The primary targets of revisionist writings were the alleged repression, censorship, and extreme dogmatism of the Soviet interpreters of Marxist-Leninist theory, as mentioned earlier by Aptheker. It was obvious that a showdown was in the making, since the criticism soon spread from the field of sociology (in the writings of Jozef Chalasinski) to philosophy (Leszek Kolakowski), and finally to the students in the universities at whom the revisionists had originally aimed their theory. Meanwhile, the students, less openly but more actively, were absorbing these glib ideas. Soon a large segment of the students, especially at Warsaw University, were solidly aligned with the "new Marxists". This alliance led to the ascendancy of the above-mentioned student paper, *Po Prostu*, reaching a circulation at one point of 150,000 copies.[15] This wide circulation seems partially to contradict the continual charges of repression and suppression voiced by the "opposition within", not only in Poland, but as cited earlier, in Yugoslavia, with its *Praxis* and *Gledista*, among others.

However, the chasm separating Communist Party leaders from the revisionists was not so much over the issue of censorship, although censorship certainly was the catalyst, but rather concerned the economic and social policies as established by the Communist Party. This distinction, as mentioned by Aptheker earlier, will also apply in the Hungarian situation.

In Hungary the main elements of revisionist thinking found roots within six months of their introduction into the University. In this case, the University of Budapest in 1956 became the source from which the political promotion of "new ideas" was to emanate – a source from which the revisionist philosophy radiated in all directions. With the exception of the U.S.S.R., Hungary had been the only East European country which had had a communist government prior to World War II, the government headed by Béla

13. Cited by Coser, *op. cit.*, p. 197.
14. *Ibid.*, p. 197.
15. Cf. *ibid.*, p. 199.

Kun, at which similar charges of repression, censorship, and anti-democratic conspiracies were directed.

From 1948 Mátyás Rákosi, a long-standing member of the Communist Party, was the Secretary-General of the CPH. In the course of his régime Rákosi was accused of using heavy-handed measures, including jailing, censorship, etc., in dealing with dissent within both the Party and the country, as Aptheker observed earlier. In fact, Rákosi later resigned, admitting to these errors and distortions.

> As for my mistakes in the sphere of the personality cult and of violations of Socialist legality, I repeatedly admitted at the plenary meeting of the Central Committee in June, 1953, and in the subsequent period and in this connection criticized them in public. After the Twentieth Congress of the Soviet Communist Party and Comrade Khrushchev's report, I realized that the gravity and influence of these mistakes were greater than I believed and the damage inflicted upon our Party as a result of these mistakes much more serious than I thought earlier. These mistakes complicated the work of our Party, reduced the attractive power of the Party and the People's Democracy and impeded the development of the Leninist standards of Party life, collective leadership, constructive criticism and self-criticism, democratization of the Party and state affairs, the initiative and creative force of the mass of the working people.[16]

With this type of revelation and admission came a response from many of the intellectuals in Hungary, most of whom were in jail for what seemed to Rákosi to be counter-revolutionary activities, such as urging the withdrawal of support from the Communist Party, demanding the abolition of *all* forms of censorship and an end to the imposition of "Soviet-styled Marxist-Leninist government" to include its fantastic mismanagement of the industrial economy as it emerged from the holocaust of World War II. With, then, the rise to power of Imre Nagy, a popular reformist school teacher who spent the war years in Russia and who was extremely critical of Rákosi's control, a compromise was made, temporarily, and both men were to share the leadership in the Hungarian government.

In the political power game between Rákosi and Nagy, there were never really any calm moments. The nature of the disagreement between the two men was ideological and often violent. Rákosi, in his rage and defensive posture, accused his opponent of violating a basic concept of Leninism, that of maintaining the leading role of the Communist Party. Rákosi warned that many of Nagy's well-intentioned but nonetheless alarming reforms (disintegration of collective farms, expanded powers of the press, etc.) would endanger not only Hungarian communism but that of the neighboring states as well (a fact that must have been obvious to propagandists of the West who picked up any strains of this conflict in Hungary and elsewhere, and

16. Aptheker, *op. cit.*, pp. 151–152.

made sure to encourage such trends). For example, Aptheker in his *The Truth about Hungary*, quotes from a book written by a top-level member of the CIA in 1949, Sherman Kent's *Strategic Intelligence for American World Policy*, in which the author discusses the particular methods of conducting warfare against an enemy, which one might assume the socialist countries represent to the United States. Writes Kent:

> Next down the line is what is termed black propaganda, that which purports to come from dissident elements within the enemy's own population, but which is really carried on in great secrecy from the outside. Sometimes the black propaganda is done by radio [Radio Free Europe and other CIA financed organizations], sometimes by leaflet, by fake newspaper, by forged letter, by any and all means occurring to perverse ingenuity. The instrumentalities under discussion thus far have been, by and large, applicable to the target by remote control; there are other instruments which can be employed only by penetrating enemy lines. This group of instruments leads off with the rumor invented and passed along by word of mouth, it includes subornation of perjury, intimidation, subversion, bribery, blackmail, sabotage in all its aspects, kidnapping, booby trapping, assassination, ambush, the *franc tireur*, and the underground army. It includes *the clandestine delivery of all the tools of the calling* [my italics]; [one ought to bear this in mind when discussing the Czechoslovakian incident in which the CP there made strong claims that a counter-revolutionary army was being equipped by the U.S. and was awaiting the right moment – Ralph Faris]: the undercover personnel, the printing press and radio set, the poison, the explosives, the incendiary substances, and the small arms and supplies for thugs, guerrillas, and para-military formations.[17]

But in spite of these constant threats and dangers, Nagy abolished the various jail sentences of hundreds of those jailed under Rákosi. The sudden emergence of these writers, journalists, and intellectual workers, Party functionaries, and others, was to be a main ingredient of the 1956 revolt.[18] However, it was the intellectual circle formed by these writers and activists, in October of 1956, that is significant for the purposes of this analysis, rather than the events that followed the unsuccessful counter-revolution.

Whereas the universities are important focal points of slow or rapid political consciousness, the *Reviews*, very often founded in university or student circles, are constant centers of ideological consciousness. Their effect is to concentrate the vague and sometimes ineffectual streams of thought which, once expressed in their essential form, are communicated to wider public spheres than university meetings and scholarly publications can reach. With this in mind, then, the Petőfi circle in Budapest (in 1956), created through the untiring spirit and activity of interested students and faculty members,

17. *Ibid.*, p. 79.
18. Cf. Vaclav Benes, *Eastern European Government and Politics*, (New York: Harper & Row, 1966), p. 150.

was to provide the students and intellectuals with an opportunity to exchange ideas and discuss problems of common interest – to include the distortions and perversions of socialist policy both in Hungary and other East European countries. What is of special importance here is that in six active months, the scope of the debate was changed and the range of the membership was enlarged. In that expansion process, the "new Marxiststs" were allowed to insert their reworked Marxism into discussions and publications. Writes Aptheker:

At the Petőfi meeting, the last before the summer recess [the summer before the October, 1956 uprising], Tardos and Déry (whose novel *Niki* was then a best seller in Hungary) made exceedingly bitter attacks, by name, upon many top figures, including the minister of culture, József Darvas, himself a writer, and Márton Horváth, editor of the Party's central organ, *Szabad Nép*. Déry, possibly carried away by his eloquence, not only bitterly attacked the entire Party leadership, but called upon the "Youth of '56" to emulate those of 1848 and "aid the people in their conquest of the future". Clearly revisionism – rather than purification, rather than Marxism-Leninism – was not absent from elements in the Petőfi group.[19]

It was in this circle that the influence of Lukács was brought to bear against both the influence of Stalinism and his supporters, Rákosi, and other Party members. Though under the threat of Party censorship, the members of this circle, along with Imre Nagy, openly attacked "Rákosi-Stalinist style communist domination"; this circle did force the CPH and its journals and publications to discuss the same problems and issues discussed in the circle, although the revisionist nature of the ideas and proposals were well understood by Party members. In time, as with *Po Prostu* in Poland, the Petőfi circle was to receive strong reprimands, and finally was censored by the Communist Party, but only after it demonstrated its unwillingness to expel the "new Marxists" from its ranks. The circle followed the same course of action as did the "opposition Party" leaders, Imre Nagy and Géza Losonczy, in that they

...played a grave role in the developments of events [the October, 1956 uprising]. In large part their efforts were commendable, but more and more their criticism became completely destructive and began to lose a Party spirit and Party sense. By the spring of 1956 these elements took their destructive and often exaggerated criticism outside Party ranks, sowing further disunity and confusion. Moreover, in concentrating upon criticism the Nagy-Losonczy group [as well as the Petőfi circle] tended to omit a positive program, thus again confounding confusion. And since all their fire was directed against Party leadership, it encouraged reactionary elements, from whom, in turn, Nagy and associates did not dissociate themselves.[20]

19. Aptheker, *op. cit.*, p. 172.
20. *Ibid.*, p. 247.

Thus, it can be seen from both the Polish and the Hungarian examples that, although the roots of dissent in these East European countries grew from errors and ofter poor operational principles through which Stalin and his successors attempted to maintain order in the face of severe economic and political crisis, to fight fascist remnants, and to protect the socialist world against imperialist encroachment, the specific expression of these grievances, "critical" beliefs, and counter-revolutionary fervor were to be found in such intellectual circles, papers, and reviews, located at and around the large universities. Although some of the causes of dissension and conflict were external to the university, they still became the foundations upon which the revisionists were to attempt to build a movement.

The dilemma was not an historically new one, since within the boundaries of an often patient and hard-pressed political structure, the "new world Marxists" had been striving to raise the consciousness of the members of those doubtful groups whose support they desperately needed, but failed to achieve. However, if the trade-unions and other groups, whose support the "new revisionists" vitally need, were undecided as to the proposals offered by the dissenters, the revisionists became more unsure, alienated, and frustrated – and all of these subjective feelings can, and did, add up to counter-revolution under the right conditions. That is, their overreaction to, and subsequent hostility toward, socialist policies and flagrant mistakes of Party leaders resulted in the ultimate abandonment of the essential principles of communist theory and strategy.

The Yugoslav Stojanović observes of the opposite side of the coin of socialism in crisis:

> The worst are those whom power makes incapable of seeing the symptoms of the waning of the revolution. They see the greatest enemies of the revolution in those revolutionaries who try to open their eyes to the entropy.[21]

Perhaps Stojanović is correct; but if that is true, one might also suggest that the "revisionists" *close* their eyes to forces stalking socialism. Not satisfied with the many changes from the past, critical evaluations, and denunciations of Stalinism and the "cult of personality" made by every one of the Communist Parties across the globe (with the obvious exceptions of China and Albania), the "undogmatic ones" still insist that the main battle today is between "Stalinist positivism" and so-called "creative Marxism".[22]

Some "new Marxists" account for the *rise* of Stalinism by accusing both Engels and Lenin of perverting the "original Marx", by downgrading Leninism to the status of a "Russian variant" of Marxism. Yugoslav revisionists, as mentioned earlier, through the periodicals *Praxis* and *Gledista*, have been

21. Svetozar Stojanović, "Against the Entropy of Revolution", *Contemporary East European Philosophy*, V. ,p. 383.
22. Cf. Kosing, *op. cit.*, p. 120.

especially active in promoting such "autonomous thinking". Expressing this mood, the Yugoslav Vranicki states: " 'It is time to completely reject the view that there is only one Marxist philosophy, or only one structure of that philosophy, and to recognize the need for different variants' "....[23] These scholars of opposition are self-appointed critics and watchdogs; they speak against the tendency in their countries to take technical advance and growth in productive forces as the index for the degree of socialism and social progress attained. This may explain why they remain so unmoved. They oppose the concept of deferred gratification in the name of a brighter future, since the sacrifices are too great, the rewards too little, and too long in coming. These alleged debunkers of the official Soviet ideology have initiated a new wave of criticism and have promoted the questioning of long-range policies of socialist planners.

The "new Marxists", then, in order to demonstrate the need for and validity of a newer, "pure" Marxism, or a return to the "original Marx", the young Marx, find it necessary to question or ignore the very fundamentals of the Marxist-Leninist model. However in the final analysis, it can be shown that the differences between Marx and Lenin are really the basis of the disagreement between the revisionists and the Marxist-Leninists, since the "new Marxists" cannot, or will not, place Lenin in proper relation to Marx. Dr. Pavel Kopnin, former Director of the Institute of Philosophy of the U.S.S.R. (d. 1971), in a clear passage places Lenin in perspective:

> Another view is that, although Lenin managed to contribute to the progress of philosophy, he was nevertheless not a "genuine Marxist". Supposedly, like Engels, Lenin deviated fundamentally from Marx. For one thing, Karl Marx was a humanist, Lenin a scientist. Secondly, the theory of man stood at the center for Marx, while for Lenin dialectical materialism held this position....
> Naturally, the philosophical ideas of Lenin were not simply repetitions of Marx and Engels' theses. If that had been the case, they would not deserve modern scientific interest. It was justly correct that Lenin raised additional problems and provided solutions for new ones. Life compelled him to move beyond Marx and Engels, thus "to revise" some of his predecessors' established theories.[24]

But still, the "new Marxists" and Western writers cannot comprehend the nature of this analysis. They ask again and again, "What's so bad about revisionism? Wasn't Marx himself a 'revisionist' whenever he saw that theory needed to be revised to fit new realities?"[25] The "new realities" that the writers continually mention are the different and distinct historical conditions which gave rise to the established socialist states of Eastern Europe; in addition, they argue that the different levels of development in terms of

23. Cited by Kosing, *op. cit.*, p. 120.
24. Pavel Kopnin, "Lenin's Approach to Dialectical Materialism", *Contemporary East European Philosophy*, V, p. 417.
25. Carey, *op. cit.*, p. 39.

industrial production, agricultural reform, etc., point to the need for *specialized* versions of Marxism for each country.

In fact, however, this plea for tailored Marxism does not even remotely resemble the scientific character of Marxism; it ignores the *pluralism* contained in the word "variant". Of the scientific nature of Marxism-Leninism, Kosing explains:

> Different points of view are possible within this philosophy, especially on problems that are being further studied and elaborated. They are the subject of scientific discussion, which facilitates the creative development of Marxist-Leninist theory. But this does not imply the existence of 'national variants' of Marxism. There is no such thing as Soviet, Polish, German, French, or Yugoslav Marxism, though one can speak of the development of Marxist philosophy in the Soviet Union, Poland, the GDR, France or Yugoslavia. But, by its very nature, Marxist-Leninist philosophy is profoundly *internationalist*.[26]

Nonetheless, the "new variants" proposed by the "new revisionists" are also deeply *individualistic* in character, and they oppose the concepts of dialectical and historical materialism, although some of the "new Marxists" flatly contest this view and profess to be but "creative Marxists".

Their theories and variegated interpretations of Marxist precepts reveal, however, the highly subjective and idealistic versions of matter and reality. "The foundation of the epistemology of dialectical materialism is constituted by the recognition of the objective world and the *reflection* of the world within human consciousness",[27] says the Bulgarian Marxist-Leninist Anguélov; the rejection of this substantive principle constitutes a deviation into the camp of idealism. Anguélov pops the balloon of revisionism when he observes:

> It is not difficult to see how all these writers, though claiming to be Marxists, in fact identify the object with the knowing subject. Thus, all cognition is auto-cognition. All these notions are but paraphrases of the arguments of subjective idealism, and the authors' pretensions to have elucidated the relation "subject-object" in a new way (starting from Marxist premises) are but neo-Fichtean nonsense.[28]

Finally, in attempting to prove the conscious deviation from Lenin's book on empirio-criticism found in the writings of the "new Marxists", Anguélov helps to reveal the idealistic base of their theories, specifically in the case of Kolakowski, the Polish revisionist:

> Contemporary revisionists are not at all embarrassed in presenting their subjective idealist conceptions as Marxist. However, considering the fact that their conceptions are inconsistent with the classics of Marxism-Leninism, they attempt to

26. Kosing, *op. cit.*, p. 121.
27. Stéfan Anguélov, "Reflection and Practice", *op. cit.*, p. 69.
28. *Ibid.*, p. 72.

extricate themselves from this antinomy by putting forward even more captious arguments. As Kolakowski holds: "Our attempt to explicate that which, in our view, is the fundamental principle of the epistemology of Marx, we are brought to a very simple conclusion: Marxism in its process of formation has formulated the matter in an embryonic state, to which, in the course of evolution of thought stemming from Marx, radically different conceptions were substituted by Engels, and specially by Lenin."[29]

Kosing, the East German Marxist, sees a cognate error in the Yugoslav Petrović's work:

In reality, however, revisionism deprives the concept of its historic content, and imparts to it an anthropological meaning. Thus, according to Petrović's definition, "Practice is primarily a definite mode of being characteristic of a definite existence that transcends all other modes of being, from which it differs radically. ...For example, practice is free being, creative being, historic being, practice is being through the medium of the future".... This obliterates the distinction between the material and the spiritual or idealistic activity, and the concept of "practice" uniting them is theoretically neutralized and can be used to obliterate the difference between materialism and idealism.
[Marxist-Leninist philosophy and historical experience]... show that social practice is not an abstract "mode of being", but the sum-total of man's direct material activity. In the course of this activity man transforms nature and society and continuously changes himself in the process. Nor is practice "free being"; it is conditioned by the development of the productive forces and relations of production of a given society and is subject to definite objective laws.[30]

Gajo Petrović, in examining the universal nature of alienation, both in capitalist and socialist societies, refers to the anthropological characteristic of alienation and insists upon its persistence in man, despite changes in the social structure and economic base. Petrović argues:

Some Marxists... have even maintained that all alienation has been eliminated in principle in all socialist countries, that it exists there only as a case of individual insanity or as an insignificant "remnant of capitalism"; but such a view cannot be attributed to Marx. Rather from his basic views it would follow that only relative de-alienation is possible. It is not possible to wipe out alienation once and for all, because human "essence" or "nature" is not something given or finished which can be fulfilled to the end.[31]

The emphasis on eliminating alienation permeates the philosophical and political writings of the revisionists, and in so doing, they commit many

29. *Ibid.*, p. 76.
30. Kosing, *op. cit.*, p. 122.
31. Gajo Petrović, "Marx's Concept of Alienation", *Marx and the Western World*, N. Lobkowicz, ed. (University of Notre Dame Press, 1967), p. 142.

serious theoretical errors; such errors are countered by T. I. Oiserman, Professor of Philosophy, Moscow University:

> This approach reduces the social to the individual, and attempts to discover the sources of all social imbalances in individual human existence; and even if no political conclusions are drawn here, it is perfectly obvious that the anticipated future of mankind is viewed quite pessimistically: nothing, no social change, can overcome alienation, self-alienation and the resulting tragic discord of human life.[32]

Oblivious to or hostile towards this plea for scientific objectivity, the "new Marxists" develop rationalizations and arguments which call for the *negation* of Marxist-Leninist theory and practice: *decentralization*. Their analysis of why the implementation of collectivization principles in socialist states has met with some difficulty begins, not only with the persistence of alienation, but also with the principles of Party unity and the centralization of production.

Miklós Almási, a student of Georg Lukács and a researcher and editor in Hungary, clarifies this issues when he states:

> However, the "necessary" character of work is not identical with alienation; on the contrary, the final and complete liquidation of alienation will be brought about through the human evolvement of work, through people finding in work the satisfaction of their own passions and interests; in other words, they will be able to realize themselves in work and not see in it some task which is alien to them. "Real freedom, the activity of which is work, is the self-realization of the individual and his objectivation", wrote Marx. This means that through work man realizes himself in the objective world, transfers his aims to nature, makes the world his own and through this also transforms himself. These liberated forms of work occur today in only a few special areas such as artistic work. In communism this will be a general tendency. But there too the difference between work and leisure will remain, and the combined role of the two, aiming towards each other and mutually enriching each other, will shape the evolvement of the whole human being.[33]

Almási's analysis of work processes and the economic base positively postulates the future emergence of the creative, liberated socialist man. This, in turn, is based upon the notion of progress continually taking place, dialectically, over the long run, through praxis; an idea found throughout the works of Lenin. Writes Almási:

> The essence of Lenin's train of thought and policy is that the alienating effect of the division of labor can be defeated by developing the natural social components of human activities, and transforming the millions into "makers of society".

32. T. I. Oiserman, "Alienation and the Individual" in *Marxism and Alienation*, Herbert Aptheker ed., p. 145.
33. Miklós Almási, "Alienation and Socialism" in *Marxism and Alienation*, Herbert Aptheker ed., pp. 128–129.

It can be seen that for Lenin alienation was not a question of technical development but a problem of social practice and the shaping of consciousness. Let us
look at a simple example. The worker who a hundred years ago was a mere pris-
oner of increasing exploitation through mechanization was in a much more alienated state than the one who fought for better working conditions in the trade
union movement. And, again, fewer fetishizing forces influenced the revolutionary fighter. It follows from our example that if the worker has an opportunity
to shape the organizational conditions of his work, if he can on some level have
a say in the production of the goods he manufactures, in the "policy" and economy of his plant, the shaping of his own conditions of living – then the effect
of alienation is immediately reduced. In this way the alienation caused by per-
forming a small part of a process, by the division of labor, may be bridged over,
and contact may be found with the whole. Personal participation in the wider
connexions – effective social action – frees man from alienation, whereas being
limited to immediate work – however comfortable that may become, and however short a time it may last – will only increase alienation.[34]

The distinction here between the revisionist proposals for the improve-
ment of the work process (in some cases, these "new Marxists" are, themselves, so alienated from the workers that they offer no strategy other than despair) and the classical Marxist-Leninist approach is crucial. Where the above
cited passage by Almási stresses the continually expanding participation of
the worker in the multi-faceted stages of the work process – in an advanced
industrial economy – *through* a democratically *centralized* planned economic
system, the revisionists place their stress upon the decentralization of the
work force and its related processes, which presumably will not eliminate
alienation even then, since many "new Marxists" believe it to be a human
constant. But what could be more reactionary or more backward in character than to revert to a quasi-feudalist mode of producing, to once again
have very small groupings of individually held land as the basis for agricultural production? Is this proposal likely to eliminate that distinction between
the city and the country that Marx talked about in his wiritings?

Further, many of the "new economists" urge, as did Ota Šik, *et al.*, in
the *Draft Principles*, for improving the economic structure in Czechoslovakia,
that competition be allowed to develop among Czech enterprises for resources and markets, with the enterprises keeping the after-tax profits to dis-
pose of *as they see fit*. This, of course, requires that, in order to properly
effect these reforms designed to increase efficiency and *reduce* alienation,
enterprises must be freed from dependence on central *plans* and *authorities*,
while production must be based *not on social need but on consumer demand*.
Writes one critic of these social reforms of the Dubcek "experiment":

The likely tendencies of production and planning under Sik's model, further
strengthens the contention that he has posited as socialism a model of privatized

34. *Ibid.*, p. 132.

high mass consumerism. As is the case under capitalism, this model of so-called consumer sovereignty is in fact dominated by the interests of the managements – and, in the West, the owners – of the producing enterprises. For what the sovereign consumer has actually been able to exercise choice over is the range of goods the producers find it profitable to manufacture, advertise, and sell at prices they set.[35]

After listening to the "new Marxists" one can only continue to wonder why they insist upon describing themselves as Marxist when the term capitalist would, from every characteristic of their theory, be more appropriate.

That the demand for decentralization of production represents a deviation from the basic principles of communist theory (never mind the attempts to install a market economy) can be seen from this passage from Kosing:

> Marx, Engels and Lenin repeatedly explained that under socialism the process of social development could be directed only by an "association of producers", i.e., the working class and its allies, through their democratic organizations and governing bodies. Successful socialist construction has proven that only democratic centralism with the ever broader involvement of working people in management and planning can insure genuine socio-economic progress. Complete autonomy of production collectives makes for spontaneity in social development and, in the final analysis, in the development of the collectives themselves. It runs counter to the objective trends of technico-economic development and hampers progress of the productive forces and, hence, implementation of socialism's humanitarian ideals. The guiding role of the socialist state and leading role of the Marxist-Leninist party are *objective necessities* in building a socialist society.[36]

Lenin was confronted with very much the same kind of proposals, due to the serious political and economic problems of his epoch – there were many counter-revolutionary forces then attempting to divert the October Revolution, that demanded more "freedoms". In addressing his remarks to the revisionists of his day who were advocating the return of self-managed, small-scale production units to increase output and instill "incentive", Lenin advised:

> It was proved that the revisionists were systematically presenting small-scale production in a favourable light. The technical and commercial superiority of large-scale production over small-scale production both in industry and in agriculture are proved by irrefutable facts. But commodity production is far less developed in agriculture, and modern statisticians and economists are usually not very skillful in picking out the special branches (sometimes even operations) in agriculture which indicate that agriculture is being progressively drawn into the exchange of world economy. Small-scale production maintains itself

35. Page, *op. cit.*, p. 27.
36. Kosing, *op. cit.*, p. 124.

on the ruins of natural economy by a steady deterioration in nourishment, by chronic starvation, by the lengthening of the working day..., in a word, by the very methods whereby handicraft production maintained itself against capitalist manufacture.[37]

From the above cited passages, then, it can be safely advanced that the "new Marxists" are neither new nor Marxist.

It is on overly strained, violent distortion of theoretical sources to state that philosophers, intellectuals, etc., who call for a multi-party or a two-party political system, for an end to political repression and suppression by the Communist Party, for the maximization of individual freedom within the proposed, modified "democratic-socialist" state, regardless of the implications for the future successes of socialism, are Marxists. It is in these specific revisions that the remnants of bourgeois ideology and utopian socialism can be detected. To Kosing, the proposals demanded by the "new Marxists" are "...an attempt to 'Social-Democratize' socialism, for it is based on Social-Democratic notions of class peace and the illusion that socialism can be built by the means and methods of formal bourgeois democracy".[38] Evidently, the "new revisionists" learn very little from the brutality of the Vietnam struggle and the hideous and fascist-controlled Thieu régime, for the "opposition within" has not understood, and, based upon their class consciousness, will not understand the exigencies of a world situation in which imperialism is still a powerful force. The inability to properly evaluate the dangers of any social-democratic alternatives in the Eastern European states, in terms of the divisive effect and subsequent loss of unifying strength that would result from the two-party or multi-party systems, is doubly ironic in that imperialist armies are camped on their very doorstep. If the "new Marxists", these opponents of a strong Communist Party, or the strong central role of this party in coalition socialist governments, e.g. the GDR or Bulgaria, are afflicted with theoretical and practical myopia, can they also be suffering from a blindness that does not allow them to witness the slaughter of millions of Vietnamese, Cambodians, Laotians and Americans, nor to view the continual attempts by Western bourgeois to capitalize on the very counter-revolutionary propositions they offer as the best course for the future?

John Somerville, in his exposition of Marxism, provides a basic explanation for *democratic-centralism* and strong Party control:

However, to build it [communism] is no easy matter. Determined resistance may be expected not only from the capitalist groups that have suffered defeat within the country in question, but from capitalist classes in other countries, who cannot help being aware of the implicit threat to their own continuity of power. Under these conditions, the reasoning of the Marxist is in a sense quite simple:

37. V. I. Lenin, *Selected Works* (New York: International, 1943), Vol. XI, p. 706.
38. Kosing, *op. cit.*, p. 125.

It is a greater contribution to democracy to build socialism, even if civil liberties must, to a considerable extent, be sacrificed for a period of time, than to allow the building of it to be delayed or jeopardized by party conflicts.

...Until socialism is built, the government and party concerned with building it will represent primarily the class interests of the working class contending against a partially defeated capitalist class. Its contribution to democracy will consist, during this period, not in adhering to parliamentary norms, but in consolidating its victory... ... The reasoning is similar to that of a capitalist democratic government, during a war that threatens its existence: It is more important to democracy to suspend civil liberties for the duration, ... than to jeopardize the chance for victory by adhering to the democratic norms.[39]

In their effort to eliminate that "deadly alienation", the "new revisionists" are advocating the *elimination* of a centralized state organization of the proletariat, and posit in its place, the anarchistic, unplanned, indecisive self-management alternatives. Read the words of two who would allow a "hundred flowers" to grow while the enemy pounds at the door:

In practice [say the Polish "new revolutionaries" Kuron and Modzelewski], a worker's multi-party system means the right of every political group that has its base in the working class to publish its own paper, to propagate its own programme through mass-media, to organize cadres of activists and agitators – that is to form a party. A workers' multi-party system requires freedom of speech, press and association, the abolition of preventive censorship, full freedom of scholarly research, of literary and artistic creativity.[40]

What more favorable environment could any counter-revolutionary or bourgeois mouthpiece desire? None.

In their haste to establish *their* "variant" of Marxism (without Leninism), they have developed little strategy in dealing with the contingencies of a hostile, imperialist, *centralized* force. They seem intent on committing the very errors in planning and fighting that Lenin so carefully documented in his writings. The central problem which revisionists have to face, especially with respect to the demands for more democracy, is whether it is possible for a communist nation to implement a party system or a political faction and yet remain communist.

A survey of the pattern of opposition in Czechoslovakia and Yugoslavia reveals the nature of the conflict. As Barbara Jancar sketches the various dilemmas:

(1) The autonomous functioning of an opposition in a communist system is relative to the degree of tension existing between the dominant subcultures and the

39. John Somerville, *The Philosophy of Marxism* (New York: Random House, 1967), pp. 131–132.
40. Jacek Kuron and Karel Modzelewski, "The General Social Crisis of the System", *The New Revolutionaries*, ed. Tariq Ali (New York: William Morrow, 1969), p. 149.

degree of economic and political decentralization. The greater the degree of tension and decentralization, the more favorable are the conditions for the emergence and perpetuation of an opposition. In both countries, opposition did not become fully defined until both factors had converged.

(2) The alignment of economic and social interests with the dominant subcultures is not a one-to-one alignment. On the contrary, alliances tend to be fluid. The interaction between party and non-party groups suggests the development of an informal type of constituency, meriting further study and analysis.

. . . .

(4) Constitutional arrangements also define the sites from which the opposition may challenge the ruling party group. The more liberal the constitution, the greater the number of possible sites [this could also mean sites for CIA fronts, etc.].

(5) Party strategy acts as an important determinant of the cohesion of the opposition. Where the strategy of *democratic centralism and party control over society prevailed* [my italics], the opposition tended to fragmentation, relative to dominant interest. Where a strategy of reform and greater tolerance of opinion reigned, the opposition was strengthened; the ruling group split on the basis of interests and objectives, thereby initiating a new cycle of division between ruling moderates and the more radical liberals.[41]

Thus, it is frighteningly clear (given the bourgeoisie's obviously careful and accurate study of all these factors, aimed at the destruction of socialism) that granting concessions to the "opposition within" will not guarantee the victory of socialism, nor will it insure the security of the present socialist nations. This is the dilemma of the historical dialectic at work in Eastern Europe: to be able to beat back the revanchist and revisionist elements which threaten the socialist order and at the same time create an environment that insures as much individual freedom and diversity *as the situation and historical conditions permit*. In spite of the concessions, compromises, resolutions, and assorted peace-keeping measures utilized by the Communist Party, in spite of the more than explicit historical, economic, theoretical, and practical explanations given for the continuation of democratic centralism, the clamor for more freedom is heard again and again. Less censorship, more self-determination, to facilitate different *tracks* to communism.

It is to the credit of the socialist states and their respectively well-disciplined parties and apparatus, that Party unity and centralized organization remains the *sine qua non* of Marxist-Leninist strategy and philosophy. Therefore the Party has been able to consistently analyze the grand word "freedom" and apply the writings of Lenin, in this case, in a very *specific* way. For they answer the revisionist cry for more freedom with a well known passage from *What Is to Be Done?*–

41. Barbara Jancar, "The Case for a Loyal Opposition under Communism: Czechoslovakia and Yugoslavia". *Orbis*, XII, #2, Summer, 1968, pp. 439–440.

We have combined, by a freely adopted decision, for the purpose of fighting the enemy, and not of retreating into the neighboring marsh, the inhabitants of which, from the very outset, have reproached us with having separated ourselves into an exclusive group and with having chosen the path of struggle instead of the path of conciliation. And now some among us begin to cry out: Let us go into the marsh! And when we begin to shame them, they retort: What backward people you are! Are you not ashamed to deny us the liberty to invite you to take a better road!

Oh yes, gentlemen! You are free not only to invite us, but to go yourselves wherever you will, even into the marsh. In fact, we think that the marsh is your proper place, and we are prepared to render *you* every assistance to get there. Only let go of our hands, don't clutch at us and don't besmirch the grand word freedom, for we too are "free" to go where we please, free to fight not only against the marsh, but also against those who are turning towards the marsh![42]

The "new Marxists", I agree, should be as free!

42. V. I. Lenin, *What Is to Be Done?* Collected Works, vol. 5, p. 355.

Chapter IV

SOME CASE STUDIES

(a) *Ivan Svitak*

It is not easy to become a Marxist-Leninist philosopher. Like every "intellectual", a philosophy teacher is a petty bourgeois. When he opens his mouth, it is petty-bourgeois ideology that speaks: its resources and ruses are infinite.

...Individually certain of them [intellectuals] may (politically) be declared *revolutionaries*, and courageous ones. But as a mass, they remain "incorrigibly" petty-bourgeois in ideology... To become "ideologists of the working class" (Lenin), "organic intellectuals" of the proletariat (Gramsci), intellectuals have to carry out a radical revolution in their ideas: a long, painful and difficult re-education. An endless external and *internal* struggle.

Proletarians have a "class instinct" which helps them on the way to proletarians "class positions". Intellectuals on the contrary, have a petty-bourgeois class instinct which fiercely resists this transition.[1]

For Louis Althusser, and correctly so for Marxist-Leninists, the struggle to detoxify oneself of the prevailing systems of bourgeois thought and activity entails, first, the knowledge of communist theory and, second, the courage and conviction to see the proletarian struggle through its most perilous and *aberrant* periods. It is both unfortunate and disquieting that intellectuals who purvey the often irrational, frequently existentialist in content, ideas of the "new Marxists" are unable or unwilling to observe these two fundamental propositions. However, although the "revisionists" balk at adhering to any "doctrinaire" philosophical or political positions, one may observe, in addition to their *generally* united platform mentioned in Chapter One, other common perspectives which constitute a well defined symmetry of reasoning and analysis among members of the "opposition within": (theme one) that the Soviet Union as well as the United States (although the United States is always viewed as possessing more potential for "freedom") represent totalitarian forms of government which are, each year, moving closer and closer towards one another in theory and practice (convergence thesis); (theme two) that recognition of the distortions of both these "monsters" is the starting point, of course, for the multifarious brands of Marxism as expounded by revisionists. For example, one may, as a "new Marxist", either reject the Leninist theory and strategy of Marxist-Leninist political philosophy or reject both the Marxist and Leninist content of "Soviet-style" Marxism, including its periods of regression, with the objection that the

1. Louis Althusser, *Lenin and Philosophy and Other Essays* (London: NLB, 1971), p. 16.

63

Soviet interpretation of the writings of both men is either incorrect, distorted, or not applicable to countries not similar in historical or socio-economic background, such as Czechoslovakia; (theme three) that the threat to man and his "freedom from alienation" represented by the advances of technology, with their corresponding distortions and corruption of the mechanisms of state power and bureaucratic systems of control, is increasing.

Thus, based upon these themes and the basic platform mentioned earlier, there is an infinite variety of quasi-Marxist, anarcho-syndicalist, existentialist, revisionist and even "Marxist-Leninist" schemes that one may adopt as a "working member" of the "opposition within". One would be tentatively correct to hypothesize that there must, therefore, be series or levels of revisionists representing the degree to which one has departed from the "official" Marxist-Leninist philosophy and struggle. The intensity of revisionist thought may range anywhere from mild disagreement with Party policies and procedures as a member within the Party structure to complete estrangement from the working class struggle and Party leadership in it, resulting quite frequently in a well publicized flight into the camps of the opportunists who vegetate at the fringes of socialist societies; an even more drastic movement can be observed of those revisionists who no longer feel they can operate in such an "oppressive" socialist environment and consequently flee into the camps of the capitalists, the road having been paved by agents of counter-revolution and espionage. This classification approach, then, leads us to a discussion of one of the most notorious opportunists, revisionists and renegades of the class struggle in Eastern Europe: Ivan Svitak – the philosopher of "socialism with a human face".

Born and educated in Czechoslovakia, Svitak received his doctorates from the Charles University, the University of Political and Social Science, and the Prague Institute of Philosophy. He soon attained notoriety as a dissenter whose loyalties were given to those who opposed the "Soviet imposed socialist régime"; after he was suspended on several occasions from the Institute of Philosophy in the Czech Academy of Science, he was eventually, with good cause, expelled from the Communist Party of Czechoslovakia. During the height of the Czechoslovakian episode in counter-revolution, when it became apparent that the CIA and other revanchist groups and agents were being soundly defeated by the Warsaw Pact powers, Svitak decided while in Vienna not to return to his native country. Instead he flew to the citadel and graveyard of world opportunism and revisionism – the United States. What more conclusive proof of his intellectual dissimulation and real sentiments regarding socialist causes could be mustered than the fact of his present position at the School of International Affairs at Columbia University, well known to most for its consistent pro-capitalist, anti-communist activities and studies – a think-tank in the mold of the Rand Corporation. Even a bourgeois, pluralist, value-free social scientist might

64

regard as suspect this Columbia University position for one who so vehemently castigates *both* world powers.

Like many revisionists before him, Svitak views his analysis and himself as having risen above the real conditions of the class struggle, the historical dialectic of ideas, the contradictions of bourgeois economics, as well as the battle against world imperialist powers, and attempts to disguise his actual pro-capitalist sentiment under the thin veneer of a curse-on-both-your-houses "philosophy", which, on the surface, rejects both Soviet and Imperialist conceptions of reality, etc. But after reviewing his writings, especially his latest effort, *Man and His World*, one discovers that, with all his critical analysis of the oppressors of freedom, of those leaders who espouse dogma and administer the powerful state bureaucracy, not one mention is made of the role of the United States and other imperialist powers who contribute in no small way to the tremendous pressures put upon socialist countries; therefore one has the right to ask Mr. Svitak what role the United States has played in setting the scene in his very own, former country for counter-revolution, or whether he believes that the imperialist forces have taken a hands-off attitude with regard to the internal politics of socialist countries. If that be the case, he would do well to read the memoirs of former CIA agents and state department documents regarding the Bay of Pigs affair, or Professor Aptheker's book on the Hungarian uprising in 1956. Perhaps Mr. Svitak would benefit from a survey course in geography – Columbia University is located in the heart of one of his rejects, the United States. If both groups of rival powers represent totalitarian threats, why did he choose the U.S.? Nonetheless, undaunted by a host of contradictory statements in his writings, Svitak grinds away at both "totalitarian" powers and signals the "dilemma" that "anti-dogmatic" Marxists and non-Marxists alike face: repression and manipulation by both opposing ideological camps. From *Man and His World* we derive the following ontological summary:

These evolutionary trends are now asserting themselves in the midst of the conflict between the élites which represent the world power blocs and are striving for world hegemony. Although these élites' ideologies claim that they are concerned with the liberation of the oppressed (always, of course, oppressed by the rival bloc), what is really at issue is the seizing of power by the apparatuses of the totalitarian states and the securing of economic or political influence in the third world. Meanwhile the competition of monopoly capitalism and state capitalism is presented ideologically as a fight to defend the freedom of man (against the opposite side), though it is purely the struggle of managerial groups for the organization of the world and for power. The world is controlled by the super-managers of giant economic, political and power mechanisms, to whom humanist aims mean nothing. The tendency to manipulation extends beyond the totalitarian states and nations in the form of a threat of war and of world disaster.[2]

2. Ivan Svitak, *Man and His World* (New York: Dell Publishing, 1970), pp. 140–141.

Nowhere in his book does he mention the name of the opposing ideological world power to the Soviet Union, while throughout his chapters, whenever he speaks of oppression, bureaucracy etc., he uses the Soviet Union and Eastern European countries by name as examples. Does Mr. Svitak mean that the U.S. has no repressive bureaucracies, no élites?

Thus it is that Svitak and his fellow critical independent, unmanipulated, above class, revisionists envision a new role for both intellectuals and workers, although the specifics of the intellectual's role are much more defined, relatively speaking, than those of the workers'. Svitak explains why the intellectuals are better suited to discern the corrupt nature of *both* ideologies and intimates at the new "political roles" for thinkers:

> The intellectuals who are willing to find their bearings in this way [refers to viewing both hostile camps as antihumanist] among the ideological blackmail and the power struggles of the managerial élites are the latent or open enemies of the totalitarian state and they are therefore rightly considered to be dangerous. The degree to which the administrative apparatuses are aggressive toward the intellectuals accurately reflects the degree to which they feel insecure. An expansion of absurdity always begins with a pogrom of intellects. At present, it is not expedient or effective or possible for an individual to oppose the apparatus openly, as a matter of principle, if the opposition is to take the form of effective action. But it is possible, necessary and effective in the sphere of thought.[3]

Obviously, Svitak would be more comfortable in the Parsonian school of American sociology or the analytical school of American philosophy, for both schools espouse an antagonistic role for all intellectuals as a type of universal law; yet both schools could do no more for the imperialist war machine of which Columbia University is the prototype. But then his associates with whom he labors against the international socialist movement could tell him more about their role, his role!

The creative thinkers, then, are to constitute a vanguard of heightened "liberated consciousness", freed from the shackles of both opposing powers; they are to direct their energies toward eliminating the obstacles to "true freedom" and "humanism" in both societies. But here is an interesting observation to those concerned with universal repression: Svitak's plans, strategies, and programs, as well as scathing criticisms, are *all* aimed at existing socialist countries, in particular, Czechoslovakia. It would seem that only they are in need of more "humanizing" political and social changes. However, although Svitak may *appear* to some as a "free-floating" intellectual, an above-the-battle humanist, his real intentions are underlined by Althusser in a general philosophical way and by a group of Soviet journalists who observed the "Czech Spring" and published their findings in a *documented* report.

3. *Ibid.*, p. 141.

First, Althusser's sound explanation for the rejection of the apparently innocuous phrase "socialism with a human face":

Why does philosophy fight over words? The realities of the class struggle are "represented" by "ideas" which are "represented" by words. In scientific and philosophical reasoning, the words (concepts, categories) are "instruments" of knowledge. But in political, ideological and philosophical struggle, the words are also weapons, explosives or tranquillizers and poisons. Occasionally, the whole class struggle may be summed up in the struggle for one word against another word. Certain words struggle amongst themselves as enemies. Other words are the site of an *ambiguity:* the stake in a decisive but undecided battle.
For example: Communists struggle for the suppression of *classes* and for a communist society, where, one day, all men will be free and brothers. However, the whole classical Marxist tradition has refused to say that Marxism is a *Humanism.* Why? Because *practically,* i.e. in *the facts,* the word Humanism is exploited by an ideology which uses it to fight, i.e. to kill, another, true, word, and one vital to the proletariat: the *class struggle.*[4]

Indeed, I suppose that Svitak would enjoy the specter of workers, mainly in socialist countries, proclaiming their altruistic intentions to the capitalists even as the CIA moves its "smart bombs" into position. In short, Svitak offers us only a disarmament, both of the ideological and practical elements of revolution and the class struggle. Cited by the Soviet journalists in May 1968, the following appeal to disband the people's militia is made by Svitak:

"If we have our rights", wrote the author hypocritically, "then whom do we need machine-guns and artillery against? [As if Czechoslovakia were not surrounded by hostile, capitalist countries and agents.]
"Against whom if you constitute the majority of the people? Perhaps the militia is required by somebody else, not by you? And why indeed should you need it?"[5]

But, to Mr. Svitak, removing the barrier of a strongly, worker-based militia was just a milestone along the rarified road to "freedom". Essentially, Svitak concentrated his efforts toward the achievement of two major objectives – one political, the other economic: (1) the implementation of a political plan which would authorize (guarantee) the existence of peaceful, competing, political parties, to exclude, if possible, the Communist Party – this to insure the permanent demise of Stalinist-type political repression and control. Under this arrangement, multi-formed political parties made possible by the strategic and unique characteristics of the literate Czech working classes would preside in a grand coalition of free political units. Benjamin Page, in

4. Althusser, *op. cit.*, p. 24.
5. Cited by Press Group of Soviet Journalists, *On Events in Czechoslovakia* (Moscow, 1968), p. 25.

his excellent analysis of the Czechoslovakian reform movement, quotes Svitak from one of his (Svitak's) *uncensored* lectures at Charles University on what is needed, and Page adds a postscript to Svitak's quote:

...There have been no structural changes in the mechanism of the totalitarian dictatorship, with the sole exception of the nonexistence of censorship. The monopoly of a single party has been unaffected; so far there is no machinery for forming a political will of the people.... There is only one aspect at the present time, which justifies hopes in the process of democratization – the free expression of public opinion. It is therefore in this area that the counterattacks of the conservative forces must be expected in the near future. These forces will call for restraint; they will offer new economic programs and new persons instead of fundamental political changes. We, on the other hand, must attempt to make the best use of the tolerated freedom with a view to making possible democratic elections as the next step on our way toward establishing a European socialist state.[6]

Page replies:

Moreover, the actual content of the reforms proposed, as we have seen in the previous chapters, contains little that is new. [Page's book generally depicts the reform movement in Czechoslovakia as reactionary and dangerous.] It is to a large extent an attempt to use economic and political instruments, concepts, and institutions *resurrected* [my italics – Ralph Faris] from Czechoslovakia's presocialist past or borrowed from contemporary capitalism.[7]

Elsewhere Svitak explains his rejection of Lenin's approach to Communist Party control and working class participation – a theme common to most revisionists:

Putting Leninism into effect in Russia led to the political triumph of the working class, to a victorious revolution and to the founding of a socialist state. Putting the same pattern into effect in Czechoslovakia, where the literate working class was already the strongest political force at the time the Communist party came into being and where it represented the majority of the population, even at the very beginning of the building of socialism, has led to clear failure. It was, and is, just as inappropriate that the party should dominate the working class as that the party apparatus should dominate the state. And it is so not because we are against Marx or Lenin, but precisely because we are for Marx and for an understanding of the historical context in which Lenin specifically adapted Marx's heritage to Russia – not to Europe.[8]

In other words, Lenin, who led the greatest revolution to its successful climax, and who had to face numerous, hostile armies from all over the world,

6. Svitak as cited in Benjamin B. Page's *The Czechoslovak Reform Movement, 1963–1968* (Amsterdam: Grüner, 1973), p. 12.
7. *Ibid.*, p. 81.
8. Svitak, *Man and His World*, p. 169.

especially Europe, was not able to generalize from his specifically Russian experience about strategy and Party policy for the international socialist movement. This evaluation makes Lenin out to be a droll, bourgeois nationalist, a narrow-minded zealot. How is it that Mr Svitak, who has led no revolution, not even partially successful counter-revolution, has the wisdom and foresight to discern these "national variants of Marxism"?

Could it be, as Soviet journalists have pointed out, that, under the pretext of constructing a new Marxist social and political order in Czechoslovakia, Svitak was determined to

> ...emasculate revolutionary theory, make Marxist-Leninist theory appear to be inconsistent and to show that it is inapplicable to the "Czechoslovak way" of socialist development.
>
> Assertions about the "narrow national character" of Leninism, about it being a specifically Russian phenomenon, about Marxism-Leninism not being a consistent international theory, about Marxist-Leninist theory having been "blindly transferred to Czechoslovak soil" so widely spread by the Czechoslovak press served the same purpose.[9]

Svitak and Vaculik, among many others in the intellectual circles in the Czechoslovakian reform movement, also demanded the dismantling of a state controlled, centralized economic system which represented nothing more (to them) than the "same distortions of socialist economics characteristic of Stalinism". After all, *everything* that Stalin accomplished, desired, or proposed is and ever shall be absolutely detested by the new revisionists – I think Svitak is confused over just who the dogmatists are. It does not matter that Stalin was not the original developer of centralized planning in the economic sphere, nor that centralized planning is a must, both as a rational, effective means of meeting basic needs in a socialist society and as a means of defeating the threats of the imperialist powers, who, incidentally, well understand the factor of efficiency and accuracy intrinsic to the centralized planning mode of production. Page, in a response to critics of his writings, concerning the need for centralized planning in Czechoslovakia, replies:

> The Stalinist model of central planning was historically the first attempt to plan national economic development on the basis of socialism. To reject the concept of central planning on the basis of the negative consequences of that model as applied throughout Eastern Europe or as clung to beyond the days of its greatest functionality in the USSR amounts to regarding the Stalinist model of central planning as some sort of paradigm or only possible model. For this there is no warrant, particularly today when computer technology and cybernetics offer the possibility of putting planning, complete with the crucial feedback factor, on a seriously scientific basis.[10]

9. Press Group of Soviet Journalists, *op. cit.*, p. 36.
10. Benjamin B. Page, "Reply", *Monthly Review*, April, 1971, p. 45.

And with respect to a strong, democratically centralized proletarian state, Lenin, whom Mr. Svitak desperately wants to avoid and for good reason, emphatically and persuasively insisted:

> It is highly important to note that Engels, armed with facts, disproves by a telling example the superstition, very widespread especially among the petty-bourgeois democracy, that a federal republic necessarily means a greater amount of freedom than a centralised republic. This is not true. It is disproved by the facts cited by Engels regarding the centralised French Republic of 1792–1798 and the federal Swiss Republic. The really democratic centralised republic gave *more* than the federal republic. In other words, the *greatest* amount of local, provincial and other freedom known in history was granted by a *centralised*, and not by a federal republic.[11]

But Mr. Svitak is even more confused on other points than the centralization versus decentralization argument.

Conceding, for example, that political propaganda, the dissemination of the bourgeois types having reached its zenith point in twentieth century technology of communications, is extremely effective in shaping public opinion, Mr. Svitak somehow believes that simple praxis will be sufficient to check such negative influences whether they originate in capitalist or socialist countries. *And* he dreams:

> Finally, as regards the question "Whom are we to believe"?: Today the channels of propaganda are extremely effective and empirical evidence proves how enormous a role they play in forming public opinion. At the same time, modern social life is so complicated that we have to take many events on trust, without being able to check their context. These two circumstances would oblige us to take a very skeptical attitude, if it were not for one comforting fact. In the most fundamental questions, where the immediate experience of working people is involved, it is possible to use sophistry, but outright deception fails. For people cannot be made to believe that black is white and that phenomena in which they themselves participate directly are otherwise than they really are.[12]

Elsewhere, he recognizes the danger to socialist states from surrounding capitalist countries, but dismisses them with the erroneous idea that only the external threats need be dealt with – naïvely, he suggests:

> The withering away of the state is a complicated social process and it was certainly doubly hard to achieve in the given circumstances, when the country was encircled by capitalism. Nevertheless, though the external, defensive function of the state had to be strengthened, it certainly does not follow that the importance of security organs had to be exaggerated and that the views of the classical writers about the role to be played by the state in the building of socialist relationships in society had to be completely abandoned.[13]

11. V. I. Lenin, *State and Revolution* (New York: International, 1971), p. 62.
12. Svitak, *Man and His World*, p. 15.
13. *Ibid.*, p. 14.

70

Thus, although he concedes the influence of ideological barrages by anti-communists, one means frequently employed by them being the disenchanted intellectuals and artistic types within the Eastern European countries, he refuses to admit to the need *for a degree* of censorship in any society, let alone the Party. It is gratifying to learn that Svitak no longer can operate freely within socialist countries – his confusion and ill intentions benefit him in his present "uncensored" position at Columbia University.

The dribble one hears from Svitak, *et al.*, concerning the specifically "Russian" nature of Leninism and the distortions of Stalinism, is merely a ruse to condone anti-Party reforms and unbridled political agitation. Gus Hall has Svitak and his friends well marked:

> To the vulgar revisionist the revolutionary party becomes "an apparatus". And leadership in struggle becomes "manipulation of masses". Marxism-Leninism becomes their "ideological tool". From this point the transition of Svitak to counter-revolution was a matter of days. On his first U.S. appearance he called on the United States to attack Czechoslovakia by military means.
>
> We can now let the vulgar revisionist witness return to his present ideological home prepared for him by the most brutal, most warlike class of exploiters in all of man's history. Here he now defends the class that enslaves and exploits more people than any other in history. Here he defends the class that exploits 80,000,000 workers, holds some 40,000,000 of its people in special bondage by a system of racism. Here he can sing glory to the class that is killing hundreds of thousands of men, women and children in Vietnam. On this ideological dunghill Svitak still crows about "the freedom of man". This is the inevitable pattern of vulgar revisionism if it is permitted to go unchallenged.[14]

Svitak represents one of the worst strains of the deadly virus of revisionist propaganda and as such deserves nothing but the coldest and harshest rebuff.

(b) *Leszek Kolakowski*

> ...The ideology of the working class, precisely because of its origins, is free from all mystifications and distortions in its cognizance of the world, which arise because of class limitations, and that, in contrast to the "Atlantic philosophers", the class character of Marxism is the source of and not a fetter on its objectivity – all these are truths familiar to every Marxist ...It is known what freedom of science means in bourgeois "democracies"... Everyone can dumbfound and deceive the people, the most anti-human theories are free to circulate. ...[15]

Are these the words of a dedicated Party member? Do they reflect the attitudes and philosophy of a communist hostile to revisionist Marxism, to Stalinist "dogmatism"? Yes. Except they *were* the words of *former* Marxist

14. Gus Hall, *Imperialism Today*, pp. 342–343.
15. Leszek Kolakowski, *Marxism and Beyond* (London: Paladin, 1971), p. 13.

71

philosopher, student of Adam Schaff, and professor at Warsaw University in Poland, a Leszek Kolakowski in a day when, to him, the Party evidently made more sense and was more "moral" than it is today. For today, we are confronted by a "potentially brilliant" philosopher of the "new Marxism", by a whining, super-righteous Kolakowski, the philosopher of "escapism" or of "inconsistency". In fact, the very idea of the suggestion that there exists a fundamental dichotomy between the revolutionary, war-experienced, Marxist-Leninist philosophy of Kolakowski and the dribbling, idealist, existentialist subjectivism of modern Poland's Kolakowski strikes Leopold Labedz, who wrote the introduction to Kolakowski's latest book *Marxism and Beyond*, as ironic. Ironic in the sense that one who considers there to be a crucial chasm separating the "young" and the "old" Marx, between what Marx said and what Engels and Lenin subsequently made of Marx, should then, in turn, be a victim of the same distortion. Forgetting about Kolakowski's change, the problem, of course, which we shall review briefly, is whether, as Mr. Kolakowski claims, there is any break between the young and old Marx or whether the evolution of the ideas and thoughts of Marx represent a clarification and maturation of his earlier work. Adam Schaff attempts to explain the reasons why such a dilemma arose in the first place:

> The very social causes and spiritual shocks which caused the defection of some intellectuals, formerly connected with Marxism, to Existentialism led to their misrepresenting the tenets of the young Marx in the spirit of Existentialism. When, in contradiction with historical facts, they vulgarized their interpretation of the views of the young Marx, it was by no means with them a question of an objective investigation. It is in this light that one may understand the ignorant attempts, made with such boastfulness and aplomb by our revisionists, to counterpose the young Marx not only to Engels but also to the older Marx. For such enthusiasts, Marx was finished somewhere around 1846.
>
> And yet it is precisely in the teachings of the young Marx that we find a firm and decisive refutation of Existentialist views on the problems of the individual. The views expressed by Marx on these problems, already expounded in the *Theses on Feuerbach*, and developed in his later theoretical works, constitute a rejection of the theoretical foundations of Existentialism – subjectivism, the asocial and ahistorical conception of the individual.[16]

Mr. Kolakowski is defeated before he even begins to divide Marxism into stages. If this is his approach to dealing with other aspects of modern socialist theory, what of his other concepts, ideas, and conclusions?

Although similarities between the writings of Mr. Svitak and Mr. Kolakowski do exist, especially those mentioned in Chapter One regarding a common platform for revisionism, Kolakowski is curiously and persistently

---

16. Adam Schaff, "A Philosophy of Man", in *Existentialism Versus Marxism*, ed. George Novack (New York: Dell Publishing, 1966), pp. 300–301.

more philosophical in his critiques of the socialist establishment, and, pursues relentlessly and religiously questions therein relating to morality and individual choice – questions existentialist in scope. Where Svitak speaks of competing political parties and the accompanying abolition of all forms of censorship in socialist countries, Kolakowski prefers instead to speculate on the particular values and ideals which should prevail in any society, on the idealistic concerns that should dominate human thinking and activity. He is resolved to reject the "dogmatism of absolute values"; and, in the manner of American politicians of the ruling class, who declare themselves to be for motherhood and apple pie, Kolakowski preaches to us when he writes:

> We declare ourselves in favour of the jester's philosophy, and thus for vigilance against any absolute; but not as a result of a confrontation of arguments, for in these matters important choices are value judgements. We declare ourselves in favour of the possibilities contained in the extra-intellectual values inherent in this attitude, although we also know its dangers and absurdities. Thus we opt for a vision of the world that offers us the burden of reconciling in our social behaviour those opposites that are the most difficult to combine: goodness without universal indulgence, courage without fanaticism, intelligence without discouragement, and hope without blindness. All other fruits of philosophical thinking are unimportant.[17]

Later in his book, in an effort to demonstrate his hostility to the "no third way" tenet of Marxism-Leninism, Kolakowski defines what he means by the "flexibility of choosing" approach that he offers in his version of "acceptable inconsistency":

> Inconsistency, in the sense we use it here, is simply *a refusal to choose once and for all between any values whatever which mutually exclude each other....* Inconsistency as an individual attitude is merely a consciously sustained reserve of uncertainty, a permanent feeling of possible personal error, or if not that, then of the possibility that one's antagonist is right.[18]

On the one hand, if Kolakowski is referring to traditional or conventional theories of ethics, the straw man he continually sets up throughout his book, one cannot *but* reject a simplification of a philosophy of living which establishes *absolute* solutions of moral problems independently of time, place and social circumstances.[19] But, on the other hand, if Kolakowski's attempt at defining correct conduct of human thought and activity "raises problems of the individual's responsibility, he does so in a rhetorical and abstract manner", in the tradition of the Existentialist. "For by removing the problem of

17. Kolakowski, *op. cit.*, p. 58.
18. *Ibid.*, p. 231.
19. Schaff, "A Philosophy of Man", *op. cit.*, p. 305.

the freedom of choice and responsibility of the individual from its social and historical context, he cannot but treat the individual and his responsibility as abstractions."[20] Schaff demonstrates the fallacy in the thinking of both Kolakowski and the Existentialist when he argues:

How has this problem [the problem of individual responsibility] actually presented itself to us, arising from recent experiences? The problem of responsibility for one's deeds did not present itself to us in a purely theoretical and abstract form, but in a most living and practical way in conflict between party discipline and one's conscience, and in judgement of those who, not motivated by any personal considerations, were guilty of evil deeds under the conviction that they were fulfilling their social obligations.
Existentialism cannot answer problems posed in this concrete way. Its abstract and subjectivist outlook is useless in relation to such problems.[21]

But the essay "In Praise of Inconsistency" is the very proof of what Schaff indicts in the theories of the Existentialists, whose influence over the revisionists is well known. This essay is simply further testimony to the beleaguered aura of mysticism and subjectivism in his work which leads even Kolakowski's best fan, Labedz, to comment upon his "naive Prometheanism" and "muddled thinking in places". Thus, read for yourself an excerpt from this masterpiece in abstract theorizing that rivals Talcott Parsons in American sociology:

For let us also carefully bear in mind that to be consistent in inconsistency means to contradict by an act (the application of a certain consistency) something the affirmation of which (the affirmation of inconsistency) is the substance of that act; in short, to fall into an impossible situation, into an antinomy.
Let us therefore also be inconsistent in our inconsistency and apply the principle of inconsistency to itself. But, someone may reproach us, only then do we practice strict inconsistency, only then do we attain total consistency in the practice of inconsistency – for if we were always inconsistent, but our very inconsistency were completely consistent, then by that very fact we would not always be inconsistent. When, however, we limit our inconsistency, that is, when we are not always inconsistent, only then do we become absolutely inconsistent.[22]

However, lest someone misinterpret my own statements regarding the idea or concept of absolute versus flexible (inconsistent) values, let us examine more closely Kolakowski's treatment of them to discern what seems to be in order. He argues theoretically about principles of human behavior, specifically about those that apply to human interaction: one ought to always strive for objectivity, fairness, courage of one's convictions, tolerance of the

20. *Ibid.*, p. 304.
21. *Ibid.*, p. 304.
22. Kolakowski, *op. cit.*, p. 237.

views of others – in short a set of ethics. In this respect, Kolakowski has nothing but praise for the "inconsistent" individual who violates societal norms in order to heed a more universal value – love. In his words, "the race of inconsistent people continues to be one of the greatest sources of hope that possibly the human species will somehow manage to survive".[23] Thus, we find Kolakowski falls prey, totally, to bourgeois theory and practice; and the former Marxist lapses into a Pascal-like stance – he becomes the clown of the revisionists.

Kolakowski might benefit from rereading his own writings concerning the impact of mass media and other forms of propaganda on human thought and consciousness. While, for instance, Kolakowski is busy with his "escapist morality", Marxists such as Angela Davis, John Somerville, and McEwan and Bowles are hounded out of universities in the country which publishes so quickly writings such as his and other revisionists'. The time to decide if he is really *with* us is now; the workers need further examples, not of *despondency* and *frustration*, but rather of decisive *leadership*.

But Mr. Kolakowski would not be deterred by such direct references to real world situations nor by the appeal for unity in the face of imperialist threats; he has developed a line of attack against the "no third way" political strategy of Marxism-Leninism, which is bogus, a set up. In the following passage he bemoans the situation – existing only in his mind, of course – in which one is accused of being counter-revolutionary *just* for rejecting the "single alternative" program of the Communist party:

> Whatever the factors leading to the disappearance of criticism within the bounds of socialism, the result would be to force any criticism into the position of counter-revolution, where it could be taken over by obscurantist, clerical social forces aiming to restore capitalism. In that event, escapism would offer the only alternative to a choice between being a renegade or a loyal opportunist. Yet to choose escapism means resigning from active participation in political life and *capitulating* [my italics – Ralph M. Faris] in the face of existing choices.[24]

One wonders why Kolakowski wouldn't feel more comfortable in the camps of the "middle-of-the-roaders", the parliamentarians, the social democrats; for although he denies the similarities between his position of an in-between loyal communist and that of a classic liberal, what he proposes is remarkably close to bourgeois social democrats.

In addition, after one reads Kolakowski's defense of *value-free* or *value-three* democracy, one can better understand his haste to *separate* Marx from Lenin, from Engels, and from the present-day programs of Marxism-Leninism. Read his explanation for the *divergence*:

23. *Ibid.*, p. 230.
24. *Ibid.*, p. 124.

This attempt to explain what is in our opinion the basic principle of Marx's epistemology has led us to a simple conclusion: nascent Marxism formulated a germinal project for a theory of cognition that in the course of the development of the current of thinking that identifies itself as Marxist was replaced by the radically different concepts of Engels and especially Lenin. (I say "especially", having in mind the extreme formulations that Lenin used to characterize his theory of reflection – of consciousness that copies and imitates reality.) We need not try to analyze all the reasons that led to this particular evolution, but there are certainly several. (In Engels' case it is obviously difficult to exclude the influence of the positivist scientism widespread in his day; in Lenin's, the influence of the tradition of Russian materialism; and after all, these only partly explain the matter.)[25]

But, as I mentioned earlier, this perspective is common to both revisionists and bourgeois theorists of the West, who conveniently borrow from the early writings of Marx on alienation, ignoring, for the most part, and for obvious reasons, the later works of Marx. Indeed, Adam Schaff, mentioned earlier, one of Kolakowski's teachers from whom he apparently did not learn enough, shows both the logical, historical errors in this position as well as the epistemological fallacies of this "young Marx syndrome". Schaff writes on the former first:

From the moment that Marx started work on *Capital* there was an agreed division of labour between them, and Engels's share included polemics in the philosophical field. Their correspondence shows that every step which either of the partners took was submitted to the other and criticized or approved. Marx not only had no objections to Engels's published philosophical views but unreservedly associated himself with them, in later years just as in the Young Hegelian period...[26]

If, as Kolakowski claims, Engels was influenced by Positivist scientism (and it is true that some of the stimuli which affected positivism also influenced the development of Marx and Engels) then so was Marx. If it is true that in 1844 Marx still occupied the idealistic positions in epistemology, close to Jamesian Pragmatism, which Kolakowski wrongly attributes to him, the same Marx in later years voiced different views.... Is it not nonsense to isolate some early stage in Marx's thought, when he was still an idealist (this is not true in respect of the *Manuscripts of 1844*, but is true for instance of 1841), and to assert that the philosophy of Marxism is idealism...? Is this not a typical attempt to oppose the young Marx to the mature Marx, based upon the tacit premise that the young Marx, up to about 1844, is the "true" Marx, whom the later Marx of the *Communist Manifesto* "betrayed"?...[27]

25. *Ibid.*, p. 86.
26. Adam Schaff, "Studies of the Young Marx: A Rejoinder", *Revisionism*, ed. Leopold Labedz (New York: Praeger, 1962), pp. 189–190.
27. *Ibid.*, p. 191.

Thus, Schaff takes aim at those revisionists, especially Kolakowski, who are unwilling or unable to consider the historical context in which the writings of Marx and Engels were derived; for "the analysis of a thinker's views, especially those which he held at a period of furious development, cannot abstract from their revolutionary context".[28]

But Kolakowski wishes to perform the role of a white knight for us; he wants to avoid being a "religious fanatic":

> The antagonism between a philosophy that perpetuates the absolute and a philosophy that questions accepted absolutes seems incurable, as incurable as that which exists between conservatism and radicalism in all aspects of human life. This is the antagonism between the priest and the jester, and in almost every epoch the philosophy of the priest and the philosophy of the jester are the two most general forms of intellectual culture. The priest is the guardian of the absolute; he sustains the cult of the final and the obvious as acknowledged by and contained in tradition. The jester is he who moves in good society without belonging to it, and treats it with impertinence; he who doubts all that appears as self-evident.... The jester must stand outside good society and observe it from the sidelines in order to unveil the non-obvious behind the obvious, the non-final behind the final....[29]

On the one hand, so long as he couches his criticism in the form of maintaining his role as jester in society, so long as he continues to deal with problems in the abstract cloud of philosophical thinking, Kolakowski is impenetrable; for who amongst us would sympathize with the priest as he is characterized above? The difficulties arise when one attempts to demonstrate that the members and leaders of the Communist parties are anything more than mortal men following the principles of a party which they objectively and scientifically feel is correct – the threat to which *is* real, is ever present, and which ironically or dialectically enough does come from professed friends of socialism. Albeit these men make their errors of judgment, of omission, they have and do violate basic values on occasion, and they do make correct decisions too; the point is that they *are* willing to make those decisions, which can only be made by those in the arena; they are willing to make those sacrifices which are necessary for the survival and success of the socialist movement. To be sure, questions remain as to *why* decisions have to be made or even *whether* they have to be made – questions which stand a better chance of being historically correct and scientifically verifiable if they are discussed within the framework of communist party leadership. Thus, if Mr. Kolakowski sees any priests within the socialist countries, they must be those mumbling revisionists uttering, as usual, the incantations of a mystical freedom, the pursuit of which resembles the classic tale of the priest searching a dark room for a black cat that isn't there.

28. *Ibid.*, p. 192.
29. Kolakowski, *op. cit.*, p. 55.

In cases where Kolakowski accurately describes the antagonistic forces in history, he refuses to take sides, or expresses his dissatisfaction at the reality of the situation and denies himself a role in the struggle. Elsewhere, the very topic of a paper by him indicates the level of Marxism that is being dealt with and by whom. The paper is entitled "Determinism and Responsibility", and is, according to the author, an attempt to "bring home the common logical situation of two concepts that are chronically presented as logically contradictory: determinism and moral responsibility".[30] In the same essay, he phrases the problem in this way:

> The question whether one can believe in both determinism and the efficacy of punishment without conflict is therefore banal; and we do not mean to substitute it for the question of possible non-contradictory acceptance of both determinism and moral responsibility – which is not at all banal and which has no obvious answer.[31]

One may, as did Lenin, evaluate a philosopher or intellectual by that which he occupied himself with in the course of his lifetime; for example, if one considers the topics of master's and doctoral papers at the University of Chicago in the early history of the field of sociology in America, one is compelled to negatively appraise the studies made during the worst depression in the history of the U.S.; aspiring, young sociologists concerned themselves at that time with such "revolutionary" topics as Dance Halls, telephone use, and the Boy Scouts.[32] Similarly, then, Lenin commented upon those theorists preoccupied with the "dilemma" between determinism and morality:

> The fact is that this is one of the favourite hobby-horses of the subjectivist philosopher – the idea of the conflict between determinism and morality, between historical necessity and the importance of the individual. He has filled piles of paper on the subject and has uttered an infinite amount of sentimental, philistine rubbish in order to settle this conflict in favour of morality and the importance of the individual. As a matter of fact, there is no conflict here at all.... The idea of determinism, which establishes the necessity of human acts and rejects the absurd fable of freedom of will, in no way destroys man's reason or conscience, or the judgement of his actions. Quite the contrary, the determinist view alone makes a strict and correct judgement possible, instead of attributing everything one fancies to freedom of will. Similarly, the idea of historical necessity in no way undermines the role of the individual in history: all history is made up of the actions of individuals, who are undoubtedly active figures. The real question that arises in judging the social activity of an individual is: what conditions insure the success of this activity, what guarantee is there that this activity will not remain an isolated act lost in a welter of contrary acts.[33]

30. *Ibid.*, p. 206.
31. *Ibid.*, p. 206.
32. Robert E. L. Faris, *Chicago Sociology* (Chicago: University of Chicago, 1969), pp. 144, 146, 147.
33. V. I. Lenin, *Selected Works* (New York: International, 1943). Vol. 11, p. 439.

Thus, Mr. Kolakowski stands in contrast, therefore, not only to Marx and his conception of determinism, but to Lenin who clearly demonstrated the correctness of Marx's position. Where does that leave Mr. Kolakowski?

(c) *Roger Garaudy*

Since, as Althusser so forthrightly states, one must work hard and long at assimilating a Marxist-Leninist perspective, it is not so difficult to understand those who once took up the struggle to think dialectically and espoused the basic principles of Marxism-Leninism, and who even became known as leaders within the parties of the various socialist countries and elsewhere, but who, owing to the precarious nature of their intellectual class positions as well as pressing historical conditions (for example, the Stalinist period, and of recent vintage the Czech Spring), have abandoned the historic struggle and joined the ranks of the revisionists. This slippage is always upsetting to all dedicated communists, for often it demonstrates the inherent dangers to be found in the activity of theorizing or analyzing from a class position inimicable and frequently hostile to the working classes. They fall prey to a host of ideological, world imperialist forces, to the increasing, unceasing efforts of bourgeois theorists and spokesmen – many of whom hibernate in or around the camps of existentialists, anarchists and idealists. Revisionists, over the long run, are often sidetracked into the arena of opportunism and anti-communism. Such is the saga of Roger Garaudy, who, although not an East European revisionist, nor a rejector (not on the surface at least) of Marxism-Leninism, has demonstrated his willingness to be used by the imperialist press and ideologies. Among the reasons for Mr. Garaudy's change of heart is his contrived theme of world socialism as having reached an historic "turning point".

It is for this decidedly revisionistic, opportunistic and empirically unsubstantiated world view that Garaudy, a twenty year member of the French Communist Party as well as a member of the Politburo and the Central Committee, was expelled from the Communist party in the late 1960's. However, in order that the record of fairness, objectivity and legality of the Communist party there not be held in doubt, let us examine the exact nature and circumstances leading up to his suspension. Francois Hincker in an explanatory article on the subject states clearly the character of the long-standing dispute between Garaudy and the French Communist Party:

> To begin with, it is appropriate to note that Roger Garaudy's expulsion, as an administrative action by the French Communist Party, was the result, in keeping with the statutes of this party and all other Communist parties, of violations of discipline of which Garaudy was guilty, and not of the existence of differences....
> Garaudy was expelled because in the weeks following the Congress he resorted

to violent attacks on the Communist Party and the leadership it had elected. And he did so with support – which he solicited – from circles most hostile to the Communists.[34]

Thus in spite of the complaints by Garaudy, of which the following is an example,

> Like all other Communist Parties that failed, after the Twentieth Congress, to make any serious critique of Stalinism, contenting themselves with no more than a superficial analysis (hastily cut short) by the Communist Party of the Soviet Union, the French Communist Party persisted in identifying democratic centralism with bureaucratic centralism of a kind which left room only for purely formal democracy.[35]

regarding the dogmatic, unattentive, heavy-handed, "Stalinist" style of the French Communist Party, he was given more than a token amount of time to discuss, debate and propose the ideas of his newly embraced opportunism. The problem seems to be, then, that Garaudy defines censorship and dogmatism as the tendency to reject certain of his basic propositions regarding the twentieth century "post-industrial" society. Whenever the Party disagreed, that was an example of dogmatism – how ingenious!

Further, it seems in retrospect that Garaudy's differences with the Communist Party culminated in an open break when the French Communist Party and others refused to bow before *his* analysis of two major violent episodes: the May-June French student-worker uprising of 1968 and the Czech crisis during the same year. Garaudy, unable to comprehend the non-participation in, according to him, or different analysis of, according to the Party, the uprising, viewed his party as reactionary and outmoded. Incredibly, it appeared as if Garaudy was supporting the infantile, anarchist, anti-communist rantings of Daniel Cohn-Bendit, the student activist, instead of the French Communist Party. For the FCP supported the workers in their demands and persistently attempted to articulate a viable set of proposals with respect to the *reform* of the Gaullist government or its expulsion; at no time did the FCP feel that the majority, in contrast to the five million workers in the FCP, of workers were demanding revolution. Garaudy in contrast, felt that at the very time *he* envisioned a possible revolutionary triumph, the main obstacle was the reactionary FCP. Thus he broke Party discipline and contradicted the party's policies – clearly a violation of the statutes. Georges Séguy, the CGT (the General Federation of Labor) General Secretary, who summed up the mood of the workers at that time,

34. Francois Hincker, "Roger Garaudy and the French Communist Party", *Political Affairs*, April, 1971, Vol. L, No. 4, pp. 40–41.
35. Roger Garaudy, *The Turning Point of Socialism* (London: Fontana Books, 1970), p. 223.

is cited by Jack Woddis in his latest book, *Theories of Revolution*isn; analysis directly contradicts Garaudy's:

> In these sharpened conditions of class struggle, some doubtful people, renegades for the most part, have accused us, in insulting terms, of having let slip the opportunity for the working class to take power....
> No, the ten million workers on strike were not demanding working-class power, but better living and working conditions, and the great majority of them expressed, by their opposition to the régime of personal power, their attachment to democracy under the slogan: a people's government.[36]

Woddis further clarifies the situation by referring to the test of objective conditions:

> But all this does not add up to a revolutionary situation. The majority of wage and salary workers still supported the reformist parties, or even those of the bourgeoisie. Although the industrial workers are strong supporters of the Communist Party, five million votes is still a minority of the total number of wage workers and their families. Secondly, although significant progress toward left unity had been achieved in 1967, the events of May-June, 1968, accompanied as they were not only by ultra-left posturings by the United Socialist Party but by hesitations and manoeuvres by leaders of the Left Federation, resulted in a temporary break-up of the political unity so far attained. This was aggravated by the activities of the ultra-left student factions which stoked up hostility towards the Communists, without whom there could be no victory against the régime....
> Thus, the relation of class forces in June, 1968, was *not* favourable for a change of social system. Furthermore, Cohn-Bendit notwithstanding, the State was in no way "impotent". Much of the administration had admittedly broken down, but the two key state weapons of repression, the police and the army, were more or less intact.[37]

Where did Garaudy stand on all this? Based upon *his* analysis and thesis of modern, super-technological, industrial societies, one which we will shortly discuss, the students and other "new left" professionals constituted a new "historic bloc" that might have succeeded in June, 1968, had it not been for the reactionary and dogmatic character of the FCP. Based upon Séguy's and Woddis' analyses, one might observe that, if Garaudy cannot properly and accurately gauge the potential versus the real revolutionary state of the various groups within his own country, how can he be relied upon to comment on the socialist movement internationally?

With respect to Czechoslovakia, it will be enough to say that Garaudy supported the disastrous economic and political reforms proposed by Ota

36. Cited by Jack Woddis in *Theories of Revolution* (New York: International, 1972), p. 363.
37. *Ibid.*, p. 362.

Šik and Dubček, and opposed the violent intrusion into a sovereign nation by Soviet tanks. In his view, it was

> quite clear that Russia's intervention in Czechoslovakia implies her radical condemnation of the attempts by the Communist Parties of France and Italy to find a democratic road to socialism – a socialism in which there would be a plurality of parties, freedom of opinion and of the Press, and cooperation and dialogue with men who, though they may not have the same philosophy as ourselves, nevertheless share our desire for socialism.[38]

In short, Garaudy cannot even be relied upon to spot counter-revolutionary forces and activities at work, and, therefore, cannot adequately defend the interests of the working class.

Thus, this Garaudy "drift toward pluralism", toward multiple parties and toward reconciliation with capitalism through reform of the FCP apparently was a product, in part, of a failure to view dialectically several very complicated socio-historical events and pressures. We are, then, presented with his newest offering to the socialist world – the declaration, at this stage in the evolution of the capitalist and socialist forces, of the great "turning point of socialism" – not capitalism. The major statements of fact concerning the most recent developments in twentieth century industrial nations as viewed by Garaudy, and, from which he develops a "new plan for dealing with them", are as follows in Hincker's analysis:

> The advanced industrial countries (1) are undergoing a scientific and technological revolution and (2) are experiencing rapid changes in their social structure (growth in the number of technicians and intellectuals).[39]

With these statements the FCP as well as other CPs have no quarrel; these statements reflect rather obvious and well-publicized occurrences in industrialized societies, and we do not deny certain of their implications of qualitative as well as quantitative transformations of the socio-economic structure. However, it is his subsequent prognostications and observations concerning possible alliances among the various groups within the occupational structure that clearly separates Garaudy's first facts from future fantasies. To begin with, there is his comment, which stems from the changing nature of the occupational structure in industrial nations, that the tremendous increase in the number of salaried and professional workers, intellectuals and technicians, which no one denies, is signalling the demise or disintegration of the wage-earning working class (about which there is disagreement). For although much research and further Marxist analysis is vitally needed in this domain of classes, the fact that one becomes a salaried employee instead of a wage

38. Garaudy, *op. cit.*, p. 126.
39. Hincker, *op. cit.*, p. 42.

earner, notwithstanding the illusory changes of prestige and status, does not obscure the fact that they still remain essentially something like workers, that is, with nothing but their (intellectual) labor power to sell – that is, the relations of production and its ensuing exploitation have still not been reversed. For Garaudy, it seems that, according to Hincker,

relations of production do not exist. This leads him,... to consider as identical two workers whose labor shows the same external technical characteristics and to conclude that there is a convergence toward identity of monopoly capitalist and socialist production if their products are obtained under identical conditions of the scientific and technical revolution.[40]

In addition, the complete abolition of the working classes characterized as wage-earners seems highly dubious, at least for the immediate future. The qualitative differences, therefore, between the workers as a wage-earning class, and the vast majority of intellectuals, engineers and technicians as a salaried strata suggest the continuing validity of the concept of working class consciousness, as opposed to an "historic bloc"; for this reason, it is believed that Garaudy ignores the fact that "the working class is not characterized solely by workers being wage earners, that is, by the sale of their labor power. It is also characterized by the fact *that it directly produces and that it is robbed of that which it produces*".[41]

Thus if the working class loses its distinct status as the truly independently revolutionary group, the communist parties also undergo a radical transformation:

From the historic bloc stems a Communist party not of the working class but of the historic bloc; from the party of the historic bloc stems a pluralist ideology and not a scientific Marxist-Leninist theory.... On the part of this new party he [Garaudy – Ralph M. Faris] calls for the abandonment of the principle of democratic centralism in favor of an organization of a social-democratic type.[42]

Not content yet, Garaudy turns his attention to the bourgeois created fear of the Golem, of the technocratic élites seizing power, of technological specialists offering the *real threat* to human growth and development. Many of the Western theorists, as well as some French authors, namely J. Meynaud in his book *Technocracy*, have expounded upon this theme: making technological change and development and its corresponding creation of a strata of specialized technicians the real threat to man's future freedom. And, it appears, Garaudy has swallowed this line. K. M. Kantor, of the Academy of Sciences of the U.S.S.R. in Moscow, sums up the "critical" thinking of Garaudy on this point:

40. *Ibid.*, p. 44.
41. *Ibid.*, pp. 44–45.
42. *Ibid.*, p. 45.

Herein lies the illusion, which is inherent in the left-radical consciousness (and which R. Garaudy shares completely), that today it is not capitalism but rather the technical organization of the intellectual types of activity that stands in the way of the self-realization of the individual. The rational organization of human activity in material and intellectual production is identified, then, with "industrial society" (whose equivalent variations would be capitalism and socialism), and the need of individual self-realization is delivered identically as with the challenges and direction of "authentic" "democratic" socialism. This is the objective sense of the significance of the scientific-technical revolution for R. Garaudy.[43]

From the above observation, one may assume that there is little difference among the revisionists regarding the quest for pluralist, social democracies, for freedoms above and beyond any reasonable assessment of the political conditions. Should the Communist parties really swallow such classic positions of revisionism that they have been resisting since the beginning?

(d) *Summary*

The basis of my rejection of the new postulates and tenets developed by the "new revisionists" does not rest upon the supreme and unchallenged authority of the Party as a validating agent, nor does the rejection of modern revisionist thinking represent a hostile stance to serious and penetrating questions regarding socialist policies and practices; but rather, the repudiation stems from the recognition that the abandoning of the essentially proven and operational historical laws of Marxism-Leninism represent a wholly unjustified view of both national and international forces and situations.[44] This position, then, clearly shows the irresponsible nature of the proposals made by the "new Marxists", with respect to multi-parties, decentralization, etc., leaving socialist countries wide-open to bourgeois influence and intervention. Further, the dangers of a powerful anti-communist propaganda campaign was seen of the Soviet Central Committee plenum on ideology which cautioned:

Under the flag of anti-communism, the imperialists are... trying by every means to carry the war of ideas into the Socialist countries. Under the cover of the slogan of peaceful coexistence of ideologies, they are trying to smuggle into our

43. K. M. Kantor, "Zur Kritik der theoretischen Konzeption Roger Garaudys", *Deutsche Zeitschrift für Philosophie*, May, 1972, Vol. 7, p. 832. Also for an exhaustive study which deals with the major implications, shortcomings and possibilities of Garaudy's new thesis see Ileana Bauer and Anita Liepert's *Die "Grosse Wende" des Roger Garaudy* (Frankfurt: Verlag Marxistische Blätter, 1971).
44. Naturally, there can be neither glib responses nor dogmatic approaches; the continual exploration of every category, concept, relationship, etc., developed by Marx, Engels, and Lenin, and those added by contemporary communist leaders and scholars, must, of course, be encouraged and vigorously researched.

society the false conceptions of the non-party nature of art, the absolute freedom of creative work, ideological vacuity and aloofness from politics, the conflict of generations, and are trying to corrupt ideologically unstable people.[45]

Doubtless, some of the "new Marxists" are sincere and honest in their penetrating critiques of socialist societies and achievements. Their devotion to eliminating the obstacles in the path of world socialism is not, however, what is being questioned. For as Kosing comments on the objective, historical situations in which such criticism is offered:

Very likely, individual representatives of revisionism are motivated by the best of intentions. But the objective result of their views and activity depends not on their personal desires, but on the content and circumstances of the class struggle between socialism and imperialism. As Lenin pointed out, 'It is not a matter of intentions, motives or words, but of the objective situation, independent of them, that determines the fate and significance of slogans, of tactics or, in general, of the trend of a given party or group'. . . .[46]

And DeGrood, in discussing this problem, asserts:

Marxists must *transform* reality, which means, for one thing, struggling *along with* the established parties of the peoples of the world. Their failures are failures for *all* revolutionary movements: dislodging existing parties in the socialist world can never constitute a "democratic" victory. Such parties transform themselves in their own dialectic with their peoples and with the other socialist countries. This does not mean that revolutionaries should not criticize these parties' positions on various issues, for that... would be undialectical.[47]

The question that now remains unanswered is: To what extent will the "new Marxists" develop a larger consciousness of the historical mission of socialism and of the role of the proletarian leadership in that struggle. To the extent that they are able to recognize and accept the scientific validity and correctness of not only the writings of Marx but Engels and Lenin, the "new Marxists" will be able to play a significant role in assisting the workers in their struggle for world socialism. If not, then they are slated to be excluded from the monumental tasks of building socialism, even in their own countries. For Marxists and various national working classes (and their allies), there can be no "third ideology", no rapprochement with bourgeois, opportunist theories, designed to distract and mislead the movement.

It has been repeatedly stressed that the success and validity of Marxist-Leninist philosophy is everywhere demonstrated in the existence of more

45. Central Committee plenum on ideology, cited by Daniel Bell, "The 'End of Ideology' in the Soviet Union", *Marxist Ideology*, ed. M. M. Drachkovitch (New York: Praeger, 1966), p. 173n.
46. Kosing, *op. cit.*, p. 125.
47. Degrood, MS *cit.*

than a dozen operating socialist societies and a host of new revolutions in progress. The fact that socialist societies exist and numerous countries will be becoming such cannot mean suppression of criticism of their development, naturally. As the West German Marxist, Steigerwald, has indicated, concerning especially the self-styled "Marxist" critics in the West, we cannot

> ...close our eyes to the massive problems of socialist reconstruction in a world that is still strongly imperialist, under conditions of an exceedingly difficult, international class struggle, and a heavy capitalist inheritance. We do not close our eyes to our own mistakes and defects. But nothing in these things justifies a flight into pseudo-radical negative dialectic.[48]

In this same vein, the American Marxist, Gil Green, asserts:

> Without doubt the building of a new society has proven more complex and difficult than first imagined. We now know that the habits of centuries are not easily shed and constantly reassert themselves in new ways. Bureaucracy, too, is a real menace and not easily overcome. Socialist countries have been plagued with bureaucratic excesses, with cults of personality and of mediocrity, and with remnants of nationalism and chauvinism.
>
> It will require deeper theoretical probing and political struggle for their eradication. But in order to do this it is necessary to see them in historic perspective and in the context of the worldwide struggle of our time.[49]

Are the "new Marxists" willing to do the same?

---

48. Steigerwald, "Herbert Marcuse's 'Critical Theory'", *Contemporary East European Philosophy*, IV, p. 346.
49. Green, *The New Radicalism* (New York: International, 1971), p. 77.

AFTERWORD

I would like to acknowledge the assistance, guidance, encouragement and inspiration given to me by the following people: Professors Stephen Schafer, David Kamens and Jack Levin, all of Northeastern University's Sociology Department, whose timely advice in the early phases of this work was vital; Professor David H. DeGrood, the Series' Editor, whose constant criticisms and reviews contributed immensely to its final form, and whose philosophy and personal life have influenced me more than I could communicate here; my parents, whose hard work and sacrifice allowed me to pursue my own goals in life; and, finally, my wife Jane, whose all-out technical assistance and help on this book has proven invaluable, and whose encouragement and inspiration ultimately were responsible for my efforts herein.

Naturally, I alone am responsible for any errors, omissions, etc., contained in the preceding chapters.

INDEX

Maurois, A., 44
McEwan, J., 75
Merton, Robert, 19, 23, 25
Meyer, Alfred, 32
Meynaud, J., 83
Mills, C. Wright, 26
Modzelewski, Karel, 60
Molnár, Thomas, 25
Moynihan, Daniel, 35

NAGY, IMRE, 38, 49ff.
Nearing, Scott, 89
Nizan, Paul, 17ff., 24
Nonnewitz, Wilfried, 12
Novak, George, 72

OISERMAN, T. I., 56

PAGE, BENJAMIN B., 27, 58, 67ff.
Parsons, Howard L., 24
Parsons, Talcott, 18ff., 74
Paskov, A. I., 21
Petrović, Gajo, 7, 55
Plessner, Helmut, 34
Proudhon, P., 24, 44

RAJK, LÁSZLÓ, 44
Rákosi, Mátyás, 26, 49ff.

Rawin, Solomon John, 46
Rieff, Philip, 18
Roach, Jack L., 23
Rubenstein, Alvin Z., 14, 37

SARTRE, JEAN-PAUL, 15
Schaff, Adam, 72ff., 76f.
Schlesinger, Arthur, 35
Séguy, Georges, 80f.
Shils, Edward, 18ff., 25, 31
Šik, Ota, 7, 57, 82
Smith, Adam, 44
Somerville, John, 59, 75
Spengler, Oswald, 20
Stalin, Joseph, 45f.
Steigerwald, Robert, 29, 31, 86
Stirner, Max, 29
Stojanović, Svetozar, 7, 52
Svitak, Ivan, 7, 29, 35, 63ff., 70f.
Sweezy, Paul, 9

TOYNBEE, ARNOLD J., 20f.

VACULIK, LUDVIK, 27, 69
Vranicki, P., 53

WILLIAMS, ROBIN, 29
Woddis, Jack, 81

PHILOSOPHICAL CURRENTS

BACKLIST

Vol. 1. Edward D'Angelo, *The Teaching of Critical Thinking.* Amsterdam, 1971.

Vol. 2. Hae Soo Pyun, *Nature, Intelligibility and Metaphysics: Studies in the Philosophy of F. J. E. Woodbridge.* Amsterdam, 1972.

Vol. 3. Paul K. Crosser, *War Is Obsolete: The Dialectics of Military Technology and Its Consequences.* Amsterdam, 1972.

Vol. 4. Benjamin B. Page, *The Czechoslovak Reform Movement,* 1963–1968. A Study in the Theory of Socialism. Amsterdam, 1973.

Vol. 5. Paul K. Crosser/David H. DeGrood & Dale Ripepe, *East-West Dialogues: Foundations and Problems of Revolutionary Praxis.* Amsterdam, 1973.

Vol. 6. Shingo Shibata, *Lessons of the Vietnam War: Philosophical Considerations on the Vietnam Revolution.* Amsterdam, 1973.

The series will be continued, standing orders for forthcoming volumes accepted.
Leaflet with full description free on request.
All volumes are available.

B. R. Grüner Publishing Co.
P. O. Box 70 020
Nieuwe Herengracht 31
Amsterdam (Holland)

1941